Shared Parenting:
Successfully sharing custody of children 50-50 in separated relationships

Toby Hazlewood

Table of Contents

Table of Contents 2

Chapter 1 – Introduction 4
   The Theory 5
   The Practice 8

Chapter 2 – The Golden Rules 16
   Doing it for the wrong reasons 24

Chapter 3 – Getting started 32
   When 50/50 isn't possible 36
   Financial Considerations 43
   When is shared-parenting an option? 50

Chapter 4 – Living with it 54
   In at the deep end 54
   In at the deep end 59
   Setting the rules 61
   Two homes, two different ways of doing things 69

Chapter 5 – A united front 76
   United in the good stuff 83

Chapter 6 – Logistics 90
   Home is where I hang my hat 90
   The freedom to come and go 97
   Looking to the future 99

Chapter 7 – The doubters, the nay-sayers and the detractors 100
   Kids need their Mum first, and their Dad second 103
   Kids need a single place to call home 107
   You want to have your cake and eat it 108

Chapter 8 – Hints and tips for ongoing success 112
   Dealing with employers 112
   Christmas, Birthdays and Special Occasions 119
   Family holidays 123

Chapter 9 – Dating and the single parent 126
   Getting used to the idea 127
   Back in the market 129
   A virtual-me 131
   Making the approach 133

    Single person, no kids 135
    Single person, with kids in a shared-parenting arrangement (to some degree) 141
    Single person, with kids in their sole-care 146
    Lessons learned in the pursuit of love 150
    Being true to yourself and what you want 167

Chapter 10 – Moving on 172
    It is okay to be good to yourself 172
    It is okay to move on 174
    To trust and be trusted 177
    The ex and the new partner 178
    Failure to protect the shared-parenting arrangement 180
    Being true to yourself 183
    The lengths we go to 186
    The blended family 188
    The end of the road 191

Chapter 11 – Dealing with the guilt 193
    How guilt arises 195
    Breaking the cycle 199

Chapter 12 – Looking to the future 203
    The Golden Rules .... Error! Bookmark not defined.

About the Author 210

Chapter 1 – Introduction

Given the choice, most parents would wish to raise their children as part of a secure, happy family unit with two parents who love each other, together in a stable and committed relationship whether married or otherwise. The media presents us with many different models of the ideal, cohesive family unit whether that is the Waltons, the Royles, the Cosbys or even the Simpsons. Regardless of the genre of the television show and the trials and tribulations that may befall its central characters the common theme is generally two parents who remain together through thick and thin, ever-present in the lives of their offspring. When trying to emphasize their stability, trust-worthiness and to gain empathy with the person in the street, senior politicians will be pictured with their spouse and their offspring gathered around them. In times of crisis, the Royal Family will make public appearances together, united in supporting each other and the nation through the challenge that has been presented. In short, the status of choice for a family is likely to be epitomised by the phrase 'togetherness'.

As with most things in life though, what we want and what we aspire to are not always what we get. I grew up in a solid family unit with both parents together and very present and involved in my life and upbringing and I received more than my fair share of love and support, coupled with lots of time spent watching TV featuring the families above, and I still managed to screw it up. By that I mean that a few years after getting married and having kids (almost in that order) and in spite of best endeavours by me and my ex-wife to make it work, instead we ended up parting. Lots of people do.

The main point I want to get across, and the key message behind this book is that whilst relationships and families break up every day, it doesn't always have to come down to acrimony, custody agreements and disputes over visitation rights when negotiating for the future upbringing of the children of the relationship. There is a way that kids can be raised with the involvement of both Mum and Dad that gives parents and kids alike the best possible family environment that can be established; namely via shared-parenting where each parent fulfils 50% of the parenting role for the kids. This is not necessarily a simple arrangement to establish and it requires considerable forethought, flexibility and resourcefulness in order to make it work. It also demands commitment on behalf of both the parents to them both doing what is best for the kids above all else. On a fundamental level, they will have decided to end their relationship as husband and wife or as partners, but their relationship as parents to the kids remains and will endure regardless. It is up to them how they adapt that relationship to best serve the needs of their children. I'm assuming that this is your primary aim since you have gone so far as to pick up this book, and if so, I hope you find its content both useful and informative. If I can make it work, then I genuinely believe anyone can.

The Theory

A quick search of the web reveals one of the best known, often quoted statistics: the percentage of modern marriages in the UK that end in divorce is approaching 50% at the time of writing. I'm pretty sure that not so long ago it was 1 in 3. Combine with this the number of other long and short term relationships that also fail and the number increases further. Take from within this sample the number of relationships in which there are children involved, either borne of the relationship, or in some cases children brought into the relationship from other relationships, or even a mix of both, and it is plain to see why this is an area of extreme complexity that affects many.

In an ideal scenario it would be a foregone conclusion that the emotional pain and suffering that is baked-in to the parting of families is limited as much as possible, and confined to the actual period of the split as the relationship is unravelled. In reality this is seldom the case. Families split and through acrimonious separations, divorces and 'tug-of-love' struggles, the desire to put the interests of the children of these estranged families first is often lost along the way. This can result in custody arrangements that favour one parent or the other (usually the mother), and which invariably will not serve the best interests of the child as the parents seek to score points off each other along the way.

The UK Government has sought to amend legislation in relation to divorce and family law within the Children Act that had previously remained unchanged since 1989. This amendment endeavoured to reinforce the equal rights of both parents in the future lives of their children by inserting the presumption that it is the child's best interests to have both of his or her parents involved equally in their childhood, except in the circumstances where this may represent a safety concern for the child. Historically, there has been a perception (albeit a misapprehension) that the law is biased towards the rights of the mother in families where parents divorce. This led to the phenomenon of estranged families where typically the children live with their mother for most of their lives, fathers pay support to the mother (either voluntarily or reluctantly via government institutions such as the Child Support Agency) and have court-decreed visitation rights that may vary from little more than a few hours per week, through to a number of days or evenings a week and in some cases, alternate weekends. A further by-product of this default position is the rise of organisations such as 'Fathers for Justice' whose numerous high profile demonstrations typically involve a frustrated father, dressed in a superhero costume climbing a tall building or structure with a banner to demonstrate their frustrations at the lack of fairness and equity in the granting of visitation to their kids. The nature of these demonstrations illustrates the lengths that people will go to in matters pertaining to their kids, labelling the struggle to play a part in the lives of their children as something that requires superhuman efforts and resilience to deal with effectively. When all rational and reasonable courses of action have been exhausted, I suspect we all sometimes wish we could call on a superhero to make it all okay.

In such an emotive area as the breakdown of relationships and the dissolution of marriages, it is difficult to generalise on a single 'one-size-fits-all' model for how things *should* be. However, in common with the changes to legislation mentioned above, the emphasis of this book is upon the merits of a different model; a better model; a model that is based around establishing the best possible arrangement based on the needs of the child, and equality in the roles that each parent play in the lives of the child; that of shared-parenting.

There are numerous complex scenarios that can exist which could not be effectively addressed in a single book, including such situations as:

- where one or other parent was not legally or emotionally 'fit' to establish a shared-parenting arrangement;
- where one or other parent did not wish to be involved;
- where a history of abuse or neglect existed within the family, and which was a factor in bringing about the split.

The above list is not comprehensive, but is provided as a means of pointing out that the presupposition of this book is that both parents wish to put their children first and are interested in learning more about how to make it work.

The Practice

The main substance behind this book is not based around the relaying of theories of the dynamics of families, nor upon analysis of academic papers written by child psychologists, lawyers or any other group of experts. Instead it is derived from my personal experience and is rooted in the things I have done, the mistakes I have made and the successes I have celebrated. Fundamentally it distils the lessons I have learned in the course of my life as a parent to-date.

My name is Toby Hazlewood, and at the time of writing I am 40 years old, a Project Manager by profession and divorced father of two girls aged 16 and 13 who live with me on alternate weeks. That may sound like the opener to an online dating profile (and it was – more on that later) but it also summarises my credentials for writing this book.

Like most parents, I count the birth of my kids as two of the most significant events in my life but I am not a 'professional parent'. My intention in parenting is, was and always will be about doing my best for my kids whilst accepting that I am no expert and that I will make mistakes along the way. If I can raise my kids to be happy, well-adjusted people then that is the majority of the battle won. Beyond that, parenting is just one facet of my life and I want to make that clear at the outset so as not to give you the impression that I think I've got it all figured out!

The razor-sharp mathematicians amongst you may have calculated that by modern standards I had kids at quite a young age. I say young advisedly since I'm aware that in Britain in the modern age, tabloids are full of stories of first time parents who are barely in their teens but I refuse to consider this the norm (and truly hope it never will be). I was a young parent, still 23 when my eldest daughter was born. Imagine my surprise when I discovered that my then girlfriend of just two and a half months was indeed pregnant with our child. To say that this was the path that either of us (my then girlfriend, eventual wife, and now ex-wife, Jo) or I had planned for ourselves, would be a barefaced lie; I was newly graduated from University, revelling in my first IT job in the heyday of the dot.com era, and she was still at University, where I had met her through my sister, her then best-friend. Whoops.

When the dust had settled, tempers had calmed, and various discussions had been held between us and with various of our nearest and dearest, our youthful optimism, enthusiasm and instincts of indomitability kicked in and we decided we would do what we could to make it work and make a life together. That was in spring of 1999.

Fast forward about 6 years to late summer of 2005 in a car driving along the motorways of northern Spain returning from a holiday with her family near Barcelona, the kids asleep in the back. After a number of event-filled years of trying to make it work, we both reluctantly reached the conclusion that our time together was at an end. Since meeting and the birth of our first daughter we had thrown ourselves fully into life together. We had taken our first two steps on the property ladder, got married, had a second child (a second daughter, this time conceived and born in wedlock), I had built my career and she had at first admirably filled the role of full-time mum and in later years started a career in the NHS. We had shared a lot of happy times, and some sad ones too but the realisation had dawned on us both that the endless events that we had built into our lives were merely distractions from the fact that we were not meant to be together as husband and wife. To this day I still say to people that had Jo not fallen pregnant when she did, then I don't know whether we would have stayed together in a relationship but she would definitely have been a lifelong friend.

Once the difficult decision had been made to end things, there followed a number of months of sorting things out, to unravel our joint lives, to sell our home and to find each of us new places to live. I look back on that period as one of great sadness, difficulty and personal challenge. We both knew it was the right thing to do, however putting the plan into action and making it happen was still extremely hard to do.

Undoubtedly the hardest aspect of all was how to resolve things for our kids, then aged 5 and 2. It was immediately apparent without really having to give it any great deal of thought that the girls would need to live with their mother for the most part; we would not have dreamed of separating them from each other, and the youngest was still little more than a dummy-sucking toddler. By that time, Jo was employed in the NHS, and through provision of some financial support from me and any benefits/support to which she was entitled we calculated that she would be able to provide their primary home. My contact with the kids would have to be built in around that, depending on where I ended up.

At that point, I was working freelance, and so regularly found myself changing employers. Having finished a project in early 2006 it seemed timely that virtually all aspects of my life should be ready for a change, and so I explored all options in terms of where I could work. I applied for many different jobs, and it seemed to be a sign that the first that came up, which paid a reasonable amount that would allow me to provide the support necessary was in Somerset, close to my sister and her partner, my only family living in the UK at the time. Whilst clearly not ideal from the perspective of proximity to my daughters, this seemed the best option at the time and looking back it afforded me the space and time to process the breakdown of my marriage, to come to terms with things and to heal the pain that was still present in the aftermath.

Jo and I agreed that in addition to me paying her monthly maintenance which was looking back on it not enormous, but the most I could afford, I would additionally collect and have the girls for 3 weekends in 4. The logistics of this were to be that I would drive from Somerset to Manchester and collect them, taking them back with me on a Friday evening, and drive them back to Manchester on a Sunday afternoon before driving myself home again. Whilst this was not what anyone would describe as quality time, it served a number of purposes:

- It enabled me to regularly see my girls with the longest consecutive period of separation being about 12 days. Although far from ideal, I wasn't prepared to go without seeing them for longer even if about 8 hours of the time over the weekend I could only see them in the rear-view mirror of my car.
- It would give Jo some respite each week to ensure that she was rested for the rigours of a working week whilst solely caring for two young kids. I realise that many more cope with much less but it is important to emphasize that for our faults and without wanting to sound self-congratulatory, we had been an effective joint parenting team, each playing an active part in our kids' lives. I'm sure I would have found having the kids on my own all the time from a relative standing start, extremely challenging as I believe she did.
- It also meant that I had a child-free weekend once per month within which to get my rest and recuperation and to build a new life of my own. Some may argue that I had my free time during the weeks, but I can assure you that 3 weekends per month of driving 800 miles, pretty much wrote off Monday nights. Thanks to an accommodating boss in my new job, I also worked flexible hours to allow me to set off for Manchester at 3pm on a Friday in a

vain attempt to beat some of the M5/M6 traffic, so my evenings were shorter too as I made up the time at work.

For all its inherent issues, the situation was as it was and we all adapted to it as best we could. Looking back on it now, I see that this was a challenging but also really significant period of my life, and undoubtedly also for the girls and their Mum. It allowed me time on my own to process the change that was happening in life and to reflect on how I felt about things and to absorb the lessons that I felt I needed to learn so I could adapt to where I now found myself in life. It also tested the bond between me and my kids, and gave me some real insight into what was most important to me.

What was most significant though in what we were doing, and what is a theme that is recurrent through this book is that this arrangement was based around *putting the kids first*. Yes, it could be argued that I should have held out for a job more locally to the girls so that I could see them more. Perhaps though, might that not also have:

- Prevented both my ex and I from moving forwards as positively as we did, since contact would have been more frequent, giving rise to potentially acrimonious and angry conversations and recriminations?
- Extended my job search, potentially harming the financial framework around which the set up was based?
- Prevented us from personal development, as we both had to quickly morph into resourceful and effective single-parents who were each individually able to care for our kids?

I am not a religious or spiritual person but I have become a big believer in fate and destiny and in life giving you what you need at times when your judgement may be clouded. Sometimes in the absence of a 'Plan A' of your own you just need to go with the flow and let life take you where it thinks you should go. Sometimes you need to just *do* without thinking and get on with it. I view the set of circumstances that life handed to us in the aftermath of our separation, as showing us what we needed, and we did just get on with it.

I also believe that a number of other immediate positive lessons followed for me from this period of time:

1) It taught me exactly how much it meant to me to have the kids as the single point of focus around which all other aspects of my life were based. The endless hours on the motorway gave ample opportunity for reflection and to look at life and what was going on. For all the frustrations over traffic jams, detours and enforced service station stops to accommodate toilet stops for the kids, I never once recall feeling any sense of resentment about why I was doing what I was doing. Certainly I spent many an hour wondering if this was the way it was always going to be but I never entertained any sense that I couldn't be bothered. Very reaffirming.

2) It made me realise the priority order of things in my life. After the initial hurt I certainly felt a degree of relief and optimism about a fresh start and I enjoyed the sensation of being single again, of having my own home, and of moving on with life. That said though, it never made me feel like any aspect of my life was more important than of my role first and foremost as parent to the girls.

This book is not intended to provide an account of my life, as I'm certainly not interesting or famous enough to warrant an autobiography. However, the account I have provided above is intended to provide the background to my life, relevant to the advent of my shared-parenting arrangement. So please bear with me for a little longer as the story continues…

The arrangement that is described above continued successfully for around 18 months. There were numerous events and developments that occurred during this period of life, some of which I will come back to later. However, after about 18 months of the arrangement running the situation could be summarised as follows:

- The girls, now 18 months older had coped admirably with the travel but were occasionally and quite reasonably expressing dissatisfaction at the amount of time spent in the car;
- I was starting to develop knee and lower back pain from spending so long behind the wheel of a VW Polo which was also costing me a small fortune in repair and maintenance bills, not to mention fuel;
- I appreciated the time I had with the kids, but the quality of it was somewhat lacking at times, and it certainly felt like the clock was always ticking down when we were together, between getting them to my home and getting them back in the car to return to their Mum.

It was around this time in a passing conversation with my ex that she first floated the idea of a shared-parenting arrangement and from then on that we started exploring this as a possibility. As was the case when I was looking for a job immediately following our separation, fate seemed to be on hand to present an ideal job opportunity back in Manchester offering a good salary and conditions attractive to a single parent, being as it was within Local Government. Throwing myself into the hands of destiny once again, I made the move and found a house close-by to the primary school where the kids were now well-entrenched. From 1st October 2007 I would enter into a shared-parenting arrangement with my ex-wife.

The remainder of this book looks at the process we went through in setting this arrangement up, and the lessons learned along the way in the years that have followed, living our shared-parenting arrangement.

Chapter 2 – The Golden Rules

The decision to enter into a shared-parenting arrangement was a pretty simple one when my ex first proposed it. I have thought long and hard about whether this was due to the time that had passed since our parting, and whether there were other factors that made it appealing. Whilst the opportunity was appealing as a means of tackling the negatives of our situation as it had evolved, I can honestly say that what was most appealing was that it would improve the quality of the kids' lives and the time I spent with them. The fact that it might actually improve the quality of my own life significantly too was a handy and welcome by-product!

The arrangement that we would establish had to be based on flexibility since we were embarking on something that was completely new and had a great potential to challenge, frustrate and test us all. I was going into a situation where for 50% of my time I would be a single-parent in the truest sense of the expression, working full time and also being sole carer for the kids. Their Mum was by now used to this role but for her there was the change that would inevitably come hand-in-hand with shared-custody where she would be getting back some time in her life, but would also be relinquishing some of the control and autonomy that she had-had as the primary carer for our kids in the previous 18 months. Whilst this was being done willingly it was undoubtedly a significant event for her. For the kids this was obviously a massive change too; I am pleased to say that they were glad that I was going to be moving back and they would be seeing a lot more of me, not just the back of my head in the car as I drove them around the country. They were also excited about the fact that they would have a new second home which they would spend half their time living in. But as two girls still relatively young, I don't doubt that there was a certain amount of anxiety in their little minds about being away from their Mum for more of their lives than they were used to.

The final area that had potential to cause complication was in the new arrangement being a test of my relationship with their Mum. By now we were both well over the parting of our marriage and had each moved on in life as single people. As you would expect, we were not what you'd describe as the best of friends but equally we were co-operative, considerate towards each other, and both committed to making shared-parenting work for our kids and for ourselves. Acknowledging all these challenges, we were committed to doing what we could to make it all work, but what was plainly apparent was that there was certainly no blueprint available to us that we could use to set things in motion.

As useful as it may have been (or as appealing as I may have found it as a 'professional-planner') there was no grand planning meeting during which we formulated the finer points of the arrangement and documented the ground-rules. In truth, in the absence of a detailed plan, we sought to agree the basics; that we would be aiming to do everything on a 50-50 basis and that we would endeavour to be reasonably supportive to each other in making this work. I definitely needed more in the way of support and concessions than she did in the early days as I adapted to the new ways of living, a new job and as the kids adapted to my ways of meeting their needs as best I could. Whilst we were looking to be co-operative, supportive and to a degree flexible in it all, it was implicit in our agreement that it needed to be an arrangement that had structure and rigidity.

This is conceivably the first bit of a shared-parenting that may present a challenge to you and your ex in setting the arrangement in place, assuming that you have reached the decision to give it a go. From the off, it was apparent to me and to Jo that what we were trying to establish was a set-up that was centred around the kids and due to this, there had to be a fair amount of flexibility in order to make it work. The difficulty is obvious, but worth stating that fundamentally the arrangement is being established by two people with at least a bit of history and baggage which, if not managed carefully and put to one side will hinder the effectiveness of the set-up for all involved. The flip side to this though is that if one or other of the parents approaches things in anything less than a business-like fashion and expects concessions, unreasonable flexibility and essentially takes liberties with the other person, then in essence the whole thing will fail too. The best way that I can think of to characterise the approach that is therefore needed is encapsulated in the principle which I have defined below:

> ***Flexible-rigidity*** – The process by which both parents adopt a flexible approach to the terms and ongoing management of the shared-parenting arrangement whilst maintaining the overall structure and spirit of it.

The importance of understanding this, and embracing it was learned in the process of getting our arrangement up and running. There were instances in the early days where there was a very real danger of reverting to type and falling back into the old roles from our marriage, and the important distinction to maintain is that we were *not* doing that, but instead establishing a new parenting arrangement and a new relationship with each other that was centered only on the kids. The best way of demonstrating this is in considering ways in which it could be (and was) tested. Consider some simple examples:

1) The children are on a Dad-week – Dad realizes he is going to be required to travel long distance for a work meeting in two weeks' time when the kids are also due to be with him. He asks Mum if she would

be willing and able to pick the kids up from school on that day until he is able to collect them from her. Such a request, if it does not interfere with Mum's plans could reasonably be accommodated by her as it is for the *benefit of the kids*.

2) The children are on a Dad-week – During the course of the working day Dad is invited to go to the pub after work. He asks Mum if she would be willing and able to pick up the kids from school on that day until he is able to pick them up from her. Such a request, whilst it may not interfere with Mum's plans is *not made for the benefit of the kids* and as such does not constitute a reasonable request.

Whilst both examples above may ordinarily be accommodated in a marriage or relationship, such subtle nuances will most likely blur the boundaries and rules for Mum, Dad and the kids and are therefore best treated differently in a shared-parenting set-up.

There are many reasons why I believe it is important to understand and embrace this distinction. The pre-cursor to the arrangement being established will be some sort of dissolution of a marriage or relationship. The parents may have just separated, or have been apart for some time (as was the case for me and Jo). In the case of married couples, they may have already become legally divorced or might still be legally married as was the case for us; as we had made arrangements for our kids' care, to formally end the marriage was administrative red-tape that was of relatively little importance in the scheme of things. In any case, whatever circumstances exist the common element is always going to be that both parties have reached a decision that their relationship is over. On some level they don't get on and there will have been issues, bones-of-contention and arguments that have been had, the history of which is still lingering.

What unifies the two adults is their kids and the arrangement that is reached must be focussed solely on the care and needs of the kids, rather than to preserve elements of their relationship, especially those that were problematic. As a couple Mum might have relied on Dad's guarantee to babysit on the first Friday of the month to cater for her girls-night-out to Zumba. In the past, maybe Dad could count on Mum to take the kids to their drama-group on a Tuesday since he couldn't stand the teacher. In a relationship context these acts may be expected as part of the general 'give-and-take' of life in a couple; they are not relevant as considerations in the formulation of a shared-parenting agreement.

The type of flexibility and compromise that is part of a relationship should not automatically carry-forward to form the basis of shared-parenting unless it is focussed on what is best for the kids. I can tell you from personal experience that during married life I came to resent the assumption that I was a willing babysitter on call at all times, merely because she had hobbies and I didn't (maybe I didn't get a chance to develop hobbies as I was always baby-sitting?) To carry forth such informal agreements, particularly following the emotionally charged process of separating, would only have served to undermine the strength and quality of the new arrangement and preserve old resentments that were best left to die with the marriage.

Whilst it could be labelled as trying to keep the best elements of the relationship and simultaneously getting rid of the bad bits for the benefit of the kids, it is essential that shared-parenting is looked at purely from the perspective of the children. To state the obvious if you could keep the best bits of the relationship and eradicate the bad entirely, then there probably wouldn't be any relationship breakdowns anyway.

> *Golden Rule #1* – Each and every action, decision and guiding principle must be based around the needs of the kids and what is best for them.

The second reason why I believe that flexible-rigidity is fundamental to successful shared-parenting is driven by the need for structure. The process of moving from a stable, happy family (I am assuming that at some point in time at least it was happy) to a more fragmented family model is a period of massive change. Change, as we know can be hugely stressful. As an Aquarian male who spends his working life organising people to do things in a structured way I appreciate the value of stability, control, and knowing what is happening and when, more comforting than most. If you don't believe me, ask any of those unfortunate enough to have suffered/entertained my ways either professionally or personally; there is nothing wrong with spontaneity and fun, just as long as they're well planned and organised!

I contend that everyone, and especially children who have had this significant change thrust upon them, appreciate the importance of structure, consistency and knowing where they stand. A shared-parenting arrangement that does not feature at least a basic skeleton of rigidity will fail to add anything to the parenting arrangement other than further uncertainty, tension and stress for all concerned, especially the kids.

> *Golden Rule #2* – The fundamental basis of the shared-parenting arrangement must be structured, repeatable, and enduring in its design to allow it to benefit the children (see Golden Rule #1) and to meet the needs of the parents

Whilst rigidity is important, so too is flexibility; I am not going to contradict myself in Golden Rule #2 and I think that whilst the words are perhaps contradictory, the spirit of a shared-parenting arrangement needs to embrace both.

Consider an arrangement where there was no flexibility; where the children are always going to be in a certain place, at a certain time, regardless of changes that may arise in the circumstances for either the kids or parents, and whether it is in their best interests or not. This is an environment where changes are simply not considered or tolerated, or are accommodated, but later punished via reprisal or other measures. What I have described here seems to conform (based on rhetoric and accounts from those in such set-ups) to the basic principles of a court-decreed parental arrangement. It also tallies with many peoples' experience of marriage, or so it would seem (forgive me if this perception is shaped by my own jaded view)!

It seems that once courts get involved, they determine where the kids reside for the majority of their time, who gets custody of the kids, how much visitation the non-custodial parent gets, who owns the decision making power regarding matters affecting their day-to-day life and who pays for their upbringing. I have variously heard of examples where a father was denied taking his kids on holiday as the mother wouldn't relinquish the kids passports at the last minute, where a father wouldn't return items of the kids clothing after a visit to the extent that the child was handed over minus a winter coat in January, and other examples too numerous and disturbing to mention. Fundamentally in these instances the kids suffer, since they are not the focus of the arrangements put in place for their care and the parents are variously using the perceived injustices and inequities as a source of bitterness and resentment or as a justification for using the kids to take revenge on their ex.

The examples described above are extreme and used to illustrate a point, that what we are looking to introduce with a shared-parenting arrangement is something that is *better* than what is sometimes prescribed by the legal system[1]; an arrangement that preserves structure and certainty for the child. Such arrangements will also reflect that when the children's best interests are put at the heart of all considerations, that sometimes circumstances do change and there will be occasions when the basic rules and structure need to flex in order to put what is best for the child at the fore. Remember, preserve Golden Rule #1!

> ***Golden Rule #3*** – In combination with rigidity and structure, a shared-parenting arrangement must be able to flex as the needs of the child and the circumstances surrounding the arrangement (either short or long term) change.

---

[1] *I should emphasize that in common with the premise of much of this book, I fully understand that in many circumstances it is unfortunately necessary for the law courts to set out and enforce the terms of such arrangements due to the inability of the separating parents to communicate effectively, or fundamentally to implement Golden Rule #1 themselves. Similarly, where unfortunate circumstances such as abuse, neglect or any other form of destructive conduct have been prevalent that would predicate the separating family as unsuitable for shared-parenting. In such circumstances, there may be no alternative other than a court-decreed arrangement. Such arrangements are mercifully outside the scope of this book and I am grateful for that fact, since they have thankfully never been contemplated within my life or that of my children. I hope the same is true for you.*

The 3 Golden Rules summarised above are those most closely linked to the principle of flexible-rigidity. However, there are a number of others that will be introduced later in this book (don't worry, they will be summarised later on too, for ease of reference). Hopefully by now though you will have sensed a recurring theme which is summarised by Golden Rule #1, the 'One Rule to rule them all':

> *Golden Rule #1* – Each and every action, decision and guiding principle must be based around the needs of the kids and what is best for them.

Doing it for the wrong reasons

Before moving on with the rest of the book I want to touch briefly upon some unwise or inappropriate reasons for establishing a shared-parenting arrangement. I've contemplated these as I've written about my own experiences and based on observations made in life. One of the certainties of having kids is that it brings you into contact with other parents and as little as you may feel you have in common with them, the binding factor is the children and the experiences they give you. Similarly, I've found that since the parting of my marriage, I've come into contact with many other parents in the same situation as me. I don't believe it's that I am suddenly encountering vast numbers of single-parents by design, more that my awareness to these individuals is heightened. I mention this as I would hope it adds some substance to my suggestions and 'rules' in that they are rooted in more than my own pompous suggestion or the vain belief that my way is the only way of doing things.

I would like to re-emphasize at this point that I am reluctant at any point in this book to position myself as some sort of theoretical expert or someone who is preachy about the subject. The basis for these rules (I couldn't really label them as 'Golden Suggestions' since that would lessen the impact, even though I'd feel more comfortable if I had named them as such) is my own personal experience. I don't have years or research in the field, aside from a little over 16 years as a parent, 10+ years largely as a single parent and the (many) mistakes I've made and lessons I've learned along the way.

Whilst there is no single formula or rigid set of structures that will guarantee success, there is certainly an underlying approach and overarching set of principles that I believe will increase the chances of establishing an arrangement that benefits the children greatly, and the parents alike. I've attempted to distil these into the Golden Rules within this book, however these are only likely to assist in establishing a successful shared-parenting arrangement if the motives for entering into it are appropriate to begin with.

There are undoubtedly many reasons why things shouldn't be done ranging from the ridiculous to the sublime. For example, I didn't enter into a shared-parenting arrangement so that some 10 years later I could write a book on it. It would have been easier to take up and master chainsaw-juggling and to then write a book on that, I can assure you. The sorts of things that I have suggested below will hopefully capture the majority of plausible possibilities, with a nod being given to foreseeable reasons they may come about:

1. *Because you think it will be a means of winning back your ex.* One of the unfortunate and yet most frequently occurring phenomena when a relationship breaks down is the tendency for one or other party to regret the breakdown and to want to win their ex back (not to be confused with 'getting back at' their ex!). I can speak through personal experience of the power of this compulsion, that even after having gone through the pain, hardship and difficulties caused by taking the bold decision to end a

relationship and subsequently to actually enact the plan and disentangle your mutual lives, there can still be lasting feelings months later that can lead you to question whether you have done the right thing.

At some point when time has passed, you start to question memories of the dark times and negative feelings you may have experienced, or felt towards your ex and wonder if that particular relationship was as good as it's ever going to get. You remember the good-times fondly and yearn for more of them. It is a common occurrence, entirely understandable due to the general tendency in humans to look back on the past through rose-tinted glasses, and yet also utterly baffling when you look back on things objectively.

When you throw in the complications brought about where there have been kids born within the relationship, the feelings of wanting to cling onto your ex and try and make things work can be magnified such that you feel you're not only risking your own future happiness, but that of your kids too. Clearly in all but the majority of cases the right thing eventually happens sooner or later and the factors that caused the break-up will outweigh those that were drawing one or other (or both parties) to split, and the inevitable split will happen. It is during the process of splitting that this motivator can be particularly problematic, where one or other party is wavering over whether splitting is the right thing to do and in due course the prospect of shared-parenting comes up. The partner who didn't really want to split up anyway, but sees the writing on the wall thinks that staying close to their ex through the shared-parenting arrangement will somehow be a way of preserving their relationship and ultimately the conduit through which they will win them back.

Whilst this is a scenario with which I can empathise conceptually, this is certainly not what shared-parenting is about. Fundamentally it breaches Golden Rule #1 in that it is not going to lead to the most-healthy and child-centric arrangement since one or other parent is undoubtedly motivated by their own needs and desires and will not be acting in the kids' best interests. In an extreme example, it may even be the case that certain conditions prevalent within the family would render it unsuitable for shared-parenting (such as one parent not being capable of caring for the kids on their own for half the time), but driven by their desire for their ex they push themselves into the role. This, of course will not be of any benefit to the kids whatsoever.

2. *For an easy life.* This is not a possibility worthy of very much discussion since it is such nonsense to think that anyone would just go along with anything as serious as the living and parenting arrangements for their children in the name of an easy life. However, I mention it since I am continually surprised at the degree of ambivalence that some people display towards matters of significant gravity in their lives! Suffice to say, shared-parenting is NOT the easy option, for either the parents or the kids. It requires commitment, devotion, careful allocation of resources (physical, emotional and financial), energy, time and selflessness. I strongly encourage anyone who might think of it as an easy way to exert their parental rights, to avoid potentially difficult, punitive and costly divorces or associated legal proceedings, and to generally just keep things as close as they could be to the olden days before the relationship broke down, is severely misguided . Their energies would be better spent thinking about exactly what is

important in their lives and how they can focus their attentions to better service these things in a way that is realistic.

3. *To save on paying maintenance or support for the kids.* This is a pretty unlikely motivator for entering into a shared-parenting arrangement and I would like to think that it would certainly not be *the only* reason why one or other parent wanted to enter into shared-parenting. I guess that the premise would be that looking from the most cynical angle one parent feels that they cannot afford to, or does not wish to pay over a sum of money to their ex in the form of support payments each month, and so feels that the preferential option would be to undertake to have the children live with them for half the time as this will be more cost-effective. I find this view pretty abhorrent for the obvious reason that it commoditizes the children and is based on the premise that 50% of the parental responsibility is primarily fulfilled by meeting 50% of the cost. Conceptually I pigeon-hole this viewpoint along with those parents who view each successive child that they conceive as being a means of inflating their benefit payment or to extort ridiculous maintenance payments from their ex as part of divorce settlements that have little to do with the children and everything to do with punishing the person who has to pay, or simply to get their hands on more money. A shared-parenting arrangement founded on the basis of finances rather than out of consideration for the children is not worth anything, to anyone. Later in this book I will also talk about my suggestions for treating the finances around shared-parenting as this is obviously an area of some complexity.

4. *Because you are fearful of reprisals if you do not agree with your ex in the form of withdrawal of financial support.* This amounts to being coerced into

a shared-parenting arrangement, or at the very least having to enter into it in spite of not feeling like this is the best thing for your kids (or you), due to financial considerations.

I have split this out from the financial considerations outlined in the point above, since what I am envisaging will be that one of a couple of circumstances will apply:
- The parent who would otherwise be the default main carer (for the sake of argument/convention, this is most likely to be the mother) is fearful that if father is not given 50% access then he will not pay his way. There are numerous other circumstances that would no doubt apply in this example (drawing into question the overall suitability of the father to shared-parenting more widely), but the crux is that the otherwise primary-carer is fearful of not getting financial assistance they're due if they don't agree to shared-parenting.
- Similar to above, in that the parent who would otherwise be the default main carer is fearful that the other parent may not be able to contribute to the shared-parenting of their children due to financial difficulty rather than a lack of willingness to pay.

In both of these circumstances, it is ill advised to consider or enter into a shared-parenting arrangement since once again, financial motivators are not solely-focussed on what is best for the children. Fundamentally the welfare system is such that what is best for the child should not have to be compromised for the sake of the funding of their upbringing, and if one or other parent is trying to 'blackmail' their way into their child's life, then they are clearly not going to meet the basic criteria for entering into a shared-parenting arrangement and are probably not fit to be a parent at all!

5. *Because you are fearful of reprisals if you do not agree with your ex in the form of withdrawal of access for either you or your extended family.* Such considerations are very real and prevalent in the minds of many parents, especially fathers in families that break-up. A scenario which mixes shared-parenting and a threat of withdrawal of access seems something of a paradox and yet I speculate that in some cases discussions considering these as two possible outcomes may well be widespread. Again this amounts to coercion of one or other parent into the shared-parenting arrangement and hence is not likely to be meeting Golden Rule #1. Fear is a powerful motivator and as is the case in many other aspects of the emotionally charged area of families that are splitting, a parent may not just be fearful of what will happen to their access rights if they don't yield to their ex's demands for how things be set up, but they may also be concerned for the access rights of their extended family. Too often, grandparents, aunts, uncles and cousins can all suffer when they suddenly cease to get access to the children of a relationship that has failed, for one reason or another. However, fear of such a reprisal is certainly not reason enough to discuss a shared-parenting arrangement, let alone enter into one. Alas, the fact that such reprisals are even a threat signifies that the terms of the relationship that is breaking down will unfortunately not be conducive to shared-parenting at all.

Having considered the ideas above, this is probably a good point at which to consider the pre-existing conditions that would lead to a shared-parenting arrangement being a viable possibility for it must be obvious through consideration of these (albeit somewhat far-fetched) examples that a certain ethos must underpin the relationship if shared-parenting is an option.

The next chapter considers the pre-requisites and positive reasons for doing it, in greater detail.

Chapter 3 – Getting started

Establishing a shared-parenting arrangement was a relatively simple matter for me and Jo, since there were certain pre-existing conditions that made it all seem viable:

1) We both WANTED to do this for the benefit of the kids
2) We both viewed it as the best possible way to preserve our joint involvement in their lives
3) Neither of us had any objections or reservations over the other party being involved in the kids' lives on a 50/50 basis and each considered the other a capable parent
4) Neither of us wanted to use the kids as any means of exacting punishment on each other, or as a tool to 'get-at' the other
5) We were both able to live reasonably close to each other, and within the same locality as the kids school
6) We both considered it a priority that our work should allow us to be able to fulfil the role of full-time parent on the weeks that the kids were to live with us
7) We were both reasonably financially independent (by which I mean that we were both able to support the kids independently of each other) and willing to agree on a division of financial responsibilities in order to make the arrangement work
8) Neither of us wanted to control the situation or have complete autonomy over the kids, but instead wanted to preserve a unified approach to parenting our kids, having equal input into key decisions that would need to be made about them

The above list is not intended as a definitive checklist of pre-existing conditions that are essential to successfully establishing shared-parenting (although for the most part they *are* essential). It is more that in reflecting on the time that we set the arrangement up, these indicated our priorities and what we wanted to get out of the set-up. They also demonstrate an underlying ethos that links to the 3 Golden Rules introduced in the last chapter.

It is worth stating explicitly that without most of these conditions being met in your circumstances, the idea of a shared-parenting arrangement is likely to be a non-starter. For example, a hypothetical scenario where one parent had reservations over the other due to a history of violence that had contributed to the breakdown of their relationship is hardly likely to be resolved by nor be compatible with that parent then being given 50% of the custody of the kids' time. Apologies for the simple example but I feel that it's important to illustrate why these factors need to be in place to make such an arrangement successful.

I would like to explore a couple of these points in a little more detail, starting with the split of time. I have based the majority of this book on the premise that shared-parenting is based on a true 50/50 split of responsibility for a number of reasons. First of all, and most simply this is my experience. My ex and I were striving for an arrangement that we felt would give the kids the balance that they needed and deserved. Aiming for the stable and structured arrangement that we knew would work best for our children, who had gone through a long period (in the minds of a 3 and 6-year-old) of spending the majority of weekdays with their Mum in Manchester, and the majority of their weekends with their Dad in Somerset (as well as significant periods each week in a car travelling between the two). It was our priority and aspiration that the new arrangement would be straightforward, regimented, structured and centred around them. Establishing this as the best thing for them (Golden Rule #1) our further aim was to establish a regime that we felt was fair and the best thing for each of us.

This is a theme that I will return to at a few points in this book. Most people would hopefully agree that part of a successful marriage is the sharing of responsibility and division of roles. As a veteran of one failed marriage I am reluctant to assert anything as 'the secrets of my marital success', but I certainly believe that this is one key to making a relationship or marriage work. There needs to be acceptance that the two halves of the partnership are equal contributors to a team where each brings something (or realistically a number of things) to the arrangement. Furthermore, it is generally assumed that both are focussed towards making the family's journey through life successful. Roles I'm thinking of include:

- Breadwinner/provider/bill-payer/financial controller
- Lover/friend/companion/confidant
- Primary child-carer/night nurse/babysitter/educator/first-aider
- Driver/logistics manager/chef/cleaner
- Entertainer
- And so-on…

Some of roles will be adopted by one partner, others shared, yet others may float between the two depending on the day of the week or the phase of the moon. The key thing to note is that in a successful relationship I feel it important that there is at least clarity of understanding over who does what, since failure to understand that leads to one of my pet-peeves; being taken for granted.

Once a relationship breaks down there is a massive and potentially stressful shift in the allocation of these roles that will usually mean that when the kids are the responsibility of one or other parent, either temporarily or for a prolonged period of time, that parent fills all these roles as both adult, and parent. In the case of my parting from Jo, I felt that whilst I was living in Somerset my role had skewed very much towards the breadwinner, since I was trying to contribute as much as I could financially to the costs of my kids' lives to reflect the fact that the majority of their time was in Jo's care, and that of Driver/Logistics Manager to ensure that I got to see them. I felt that I had an abundance of time to fulfil the domestic activities and a reasonable amount of time to relax and recuperate, but of course spent much of the time missing my kids. I also fulfilled other roles for myself, in keeping my own home and my life ticking over. Jo would doubtless speak to the dominance of the Primary Child-carer role in her life at that time and the lack of time she felt she had to recharge from the extended periods within which she was solely responsible for the kids. The key point in this is to emphasize that neither of us had what we felt was balance in our lives.

When moving into a shared-parenting arrangement it was important for us both, having first established that Golden Rule #1 was being met, that we should then be in a position to ensure that the arrangement would allow each of us to live a life that enabled us to be the best and happiest people we could be and hence the best and happiest parents we could be too. This all sounds a bit utopian and rose-tinted, but I contend it is a simple fact. A happy father (or mother) in a solid relationship will feel like they are supported, like they can take some 'time-out' from family life if they need to recharge if only through being given a few hours of free-time by their spouse to escape the challenges of family life after a stressful day. A kindly word, a loving gesture or simply the preparation of their favourite meal can be all it takes to ease the pressure. In a separated family this kind of reactive, short-notice gesture is not feasible. I can only speak to the personal experience that comfort and reassurance are sometimes taken from the notion that when the kids are driving you up the wall, at least in a few days you know they will be back with their Mum. It adds perspective, it gives the opportunity for regular *structured* respite, and it allows you to recharge.

And so, returning to the original point, Jo and I felt that one of the key facets of our shared-parenting would be to strive for a 50/50 split of the kids' time, both for their benefit, for the sake of fairness and equity and for our individual benefits too.

> ***Golden Rule #4*** – Once Golden Rule #1 has been satisfied, it is okay for the shared-parenting arrangement to be designed for the mutual and individual benefit of the parents. Ensure though that it is equally beneficial otherwise resentments and negativity will creep in.

When 50/50 isn't possible

By virtue of the fact that I have written a book on the subject it hopefully won't come as any surprise to you that I speak to a lot of people about families, parenting and their approach to child rearing. I will discuss later the views I've encountered on the subject of shared-parenting but it is worth pointing out that many feel that there are numerous barriers to it that simply wouldn't make it work for them. Part of my motivation in those conversations, and therefore in this book is to understand if these really are barriers.

There are many legitimate reasons why a 50/50 split may or may not be feasible for a family. Whilst a 50/50 split would probably be deemed the most literal interpretation of shared-parenting, it may simply not fit the needs of the children or the parents. A few examples are considered below.

The first of these is in the instance where one parent has moved away following the split, or where the parents no longer both live in the same locality as the kids' school. Under these circumstances it is probably difficult to establish a shared-parenting arrangement in the truest sense of the word since it will presumably be difficult to provide the consistent elements of home life that such an arrangement demands; first and foremost, the ability for the child to move seamlessly between their homes and attend the same school, be near their friends and to have a reasonable amount of stability throughout their lives. That is not to say that this cannot be catered for depending on the determination, financial means and job-flexibility of the parents in such circumstances, but generally speaking distance will give rise to difficulty.

At an early stage before I had committed to moving back to Manchester I explored the notion of taking a rental property in Manchester as a second home that I would use on alternate weeks, so as to be able to have the kids with me in a shared-parenting arrangement and to work from Manchester during those weeks. My reasoning was that I would only require a one-bedroomed apartment (the girls could share the bedroom and I could make do with a sofa-bed) and this could be cost-effective in reducing the travel involved for all. I have to say though that looking back on this idea I am glad that it was not taken any further. The main reasons why I say this are as follows:

- Whilst this would have reduced my travelling each month by a little bit, it was still going to mean my life was lived out of two places;
- Although the girls would have had a second home in Manchester I strongly suspect that this would have challenged my financial means to the point that I couldn't have made the best of the extended time I did have with them;
- It might not necessarily have proven to be acceptable to my employer;
- There would have been an overall sense of the arrangement being 'temporary';

- My quality of life wouldn't have been as good as it could have been (breaching Golden Rule #4) which would probably have limited the benefit that it could have had for the kids (breaching Golden Rule #1).

This does only represent my experience and the different arrangements which I considered. Whilst a scenario whereby the two parents do not live in reasonably close proximity can be accommodated under a shared-parenting arrangement (I am reluctant to offer a distance, but suggest that the kids must be able to easily commute to school from both homes), then it will probably be prohibitively difficult to make an arrangement work. That is not to say that a co-operative and equitable arrangement can't be agreed between the parents but this is not likely to fit into our definition of a shared-parenting arrangement, or not on a 50/50 basis at least. The above, leads me on to the definition of our next golden rule.

> *Golden Rule #5* – In agreeing the terms of a shared-parenting arrangement, there must be a consideration of the overall sustainability of the arrangement and the effects it will have on the quality of life of the kids and the parents. If the terms of the arrangement require excessive compromise, expenditure, travel, or efforts to be made on a long-term basis then it is likely that the arrangement will at some point cease to work for everyone and may ultimately fail.

A further circumstance where 50/50 may not be feasible is where the parents work different patterns of employment. I have debated about whether to include this section or not, since there are potentially so many permutations and combinations of working patterns that two parents may have, it could be excessively time-consuming to consider the relative merits of each, only one of which will presumably apply to each reader. For the purposes of completeness, I have included a couple of illustrative scenarios to demonstrate how this factor can influence things and trust that you will be able to foresee the appropriate aspects that may apply to you.

> *Scenario 1 – Mum works full-time, standard office hours; Dad works full-time, shift hours (including nights and weekends).*

This scenario offers some immediate challenges to that where both parents are able to fulfil their child-care needs either through school hours or traditional child-care options. I think that through resilience and determination combined with a bit of luck, most parents can find a way of accommodating the rigours of child-care in the modern world of work through use of breakfast clubs, after school clubs, nurseries, child-minders and assistance from friends and family.

The best possible way to accommodate this scenario is that Dad must attempt to have his working patterns aligned with his child-care commitments such that his anti-social hours are worked when he doesn't have the kids. I will come back to the topic of managing working relationships later in the book, however I think both parents need to adopt the mind-set that for the weeks they have the kids, they are a parent first and <insert vocation here> second. This doesn't mean that things will always work in Dad's favour when shifts are being allocated, and indeed there will doubtless be times when things need to be juggled around. However, the alternative where the shared-parenting arrangement is not based on a fair or consistent footing, where Mum is constantly flexing the days that she will have the kids to accommodate Dad's shifts and the kids have no real clarity on where they will be from one week to the next is in breach of Golden Rule #2 and may well lead to failure of the arrangement.

I have known families where both the shift-working of one or other parent is 'managed' with employers, and where the shift-worker is basically dictated to by their employer as to when they will work or not, which is then in turn dictated onwards to the other parent. Based on the observation of both scenarios my recommendation above is borne out in this (albeit relatively small) sample; shift patterns do need to be managed by the shift-worker.

To summarise then, I believe that different working patterns can be accommodated if both parents are willing to prioritise their availability for being a parent, or adopt a structured pattern of childcare during the weeks they have the kids to ensure that there is little variation from week to week for the kids.

> *Scenario 2 – Mum works full-time, from varying locations around the country; Dad works full-time from an office near home, but occasionally has to travel on long day-trips for work.*

The immediate challenge offered here is in what would happen to the kids in either circumstance where Mum needed to stay away in a week where the kids were with her, or where Dad needed to travel to a meeting in a week where the kids were with him. This is also the scenario which best fits my own personal circumstances and shared-parenting agreement, so I speak from experience.

The key success factor in adapting this situation into a shared-parenting arrangement is in the parents respectively prioritising the weeks when the kids are with them upon actually being at home, and planning working calendars around making this the case. For Mum, this demands the necessity to plan ahead her travelling schedule as far as possible to ensure that she travels only in the weeks when the kids are not with her. For Dad, out-of-town business meetings are also planned for his kids-free weeks. It is only through adopting this approach that

Golden Rule #2, of maintaining a repeatable and structured pattern can be preserved. Of course, within bounds there is also scope for flexibility to be sought by either parent (Golden Rule #3) in the odd-instance where a last minute, emergency or extremely important meeting or business trip comes up. I would suggest that this is done as the exception rather than the rule, and that the structure of the shared-parenting arrangement is prioritised and preserved rigorously where possible.

In a modern family (either with parents who are together, or apart) both parents are equally likely to be actively seeking professional careers and it is not unreasonable to expect that both Mum and Dad are likely to want to be able to embrace this with the travel demands that may be placed upon them. Such careers are likely to be challenging and fulfilling (hence leading to happy parents) and financially rewarding (hence leading to parents able to independently provide for their children) and so as with any work situation they are to be encouraged and supported *where possible* via the shared-parenting arrangement. The word of caution in relation to this scenario is to emphasize that the onus is still upon each parent to prioritise with their employer, and with the management of their professional diary that any potential disruptions to their shared-parenting arrangement are minimised, *not* to rely on their ex to pick up loose ends and support them in the first instance. Without this focus, the integrity of the arrangement will be compromised since the rigour and structure of it will not be sustainable and there will be a real danger of an over-reliance between Mum and Dad on each other. This in turn will risk undermining the effectiveness and spirit of the shared-parenting arrangement through eroding and potentially breaching Golden Rule #3. Proceed with caution.

There are undoubtedly many other variations of working commitments that will have different impacts upon the shared-parenting arrangement that you establish. I hope that the scenarios above demonstrate some of the basic principles that need to be applied to determine how these influences are accommodated and managed, namely:

- Golden Rule #1 – Is the arrangement being implemented for the benefit of the kids, or is this really focussed on (for example) fostering the best conditions for the furthering of Mum's or Dad's individual careers?
- Golden Rule #2 – Is it going to be possible to establish an arrangement with sufficient structure, reliability and repeatability such that the kids will know where they're going to be from one week to the next or are the kids going to never have 2 weeks that are the same due to the ever-changing nature and demands of their parents' jobs?
- Golden Rule #3 – Is there going to be an excessive reliance on a regular basis from Mum or Dad on the other parent to 'cover for them' at short notice, effectively undermining the effectiveness of the shared-parenting arrangement?

It is only through answering these questions fully, honestly and openly that Mum and Dad will be able to determine if a shared-parenting arrangement is possible, and if so, whether a 50/50 split is appropriate or viable. It may be that 50/50 is not possible but that another arrangement suits better, (e.g. 60/40, where one parent works part time and the other full-time), however, the true test of the viability of any arrangement will always come through its evaluation against the Golden Rules. Give it a try!

Financial Considerations

The next area to touch upon is in the financial considerations associated with a shared-parenting arrangement. As with the discussion above around the best way of splitting custody I will start from the premise that both parents are interested in equity, fairness and wanting everything to be even (which of course, it seldom is!)

In an ideal world and in the spirit of a fair and equitable split, both parents would be responsible for 50% of the costs associated with their kids. This would mean that each parent paid for the kids during the time they were with them, and no money would need to change hands between the parents to set things straight. In reality this is unlikely to be the case. Additionally, as any parent will know the financial expenditures demanded by kids aren't constrained to those associated with their day-to-day keep, but that there are always forthcoming school trips, clothes, shoes, presents (for them and their friends when the kids are of party-going age), pocket-money and so-on. I used to think it was simple, but am actually convinced that things are getting more complex for parents as the years go by; consider the funding of mobile-phone credits, website subscriptions (for the latest online gaming site or app) and how these are funded alongside or instead of pocket-money... It's an economy in its own right!

Obviously it will depend on the circumstances within the family that is splitting, especially factors such as age of the kids and the employment situations of each parent as to how easy it is to design a financial arrangement that is considered fair and equitable by all involved. Again, the possible number of combinations and scenarios arising in this instance is numerous and therefore massively complex to consider. Some example scenarios may be of use in illustrating this complexity:

- One parent works full-time, the other is full-time child-carer at home (one or more of the kids is therefore presumed to be of pre-school age)
- Both parents work full-time, (the kids are in full-time education or full-time childcare)
- One parent works full-time, the other works part-time (one child is at school full-time, the other part time and at home with the parent the rest of the time)
- And so-on...

As is quickly apparent, there could be numerous different scenarios and combinations of employment situation, and the financial aspects of the parenting-arrangement would doubtless be different for each. Indeed, the financial aspects of the separation/divorce are likely to be the most complex and potentially emotive aspects to resolve (after the arrangements for the kids of course!). Instead of considering each scenario, I would instead like to propose a rule of thumb, that is based on a number of assumptions that outline what are the most practical steps for addressing this complex area.

First, a few assumptions:

1) In the spirit of Golden Rule #1, it is assumed that the parents want to arrive at a financial support arrangement that is based around what is best for the kids.
2) Similarly, it will be important that Golden Rule #4 must also be satisfied in that the arrangement must also work for and be acceptable to both parents to allow them to move forward as individuals in life.
3) Golden Rule #5 must also be satisfied to ensure that the arrangement is sustainable in the long term, otherwise there is a danger of resentment

creeping in on behalf of either parent and subsequently danger that the arrangement will fail.

4) Given that the parents are entering into a co-operative and fair arrangement for the benefit of their kids, it is assumed that they have adopted a similar approach in relation to resolving and separating their joint finances. As such, any financial considerations made at this point are solely in relation to the kids and matters such as what happens to ownership/tenancy of the former family-home, sharing of savings and investments and responsibility for any debt resulting from the relationship have been or will be resolved separately.

5) In the brave-new-world that both parents are entering into it is assumed that both will be striving for a degree of financial independence from each other. The reality of becoming a single parent is that one needs to attain a level of financial self-sufficiency whether by taking on a new job, extending working hours, applying for support via benefits and/or agreeing a financial support package with their ex (see 3 above). This assumption is separated from 3 above since it is more about the spirit of independence being present rather than the practical establishing of it.

Assuming that the above statements broadly apply to you and your ex, the process of agreeing the financial elements of the shared-parenting agreement become relatively simple. Let me illustrate via the process that Jo and I went through.

Stage 1 – When we first separated. Our collective purpose in addressing financial matters when we parted, aside from navigating what was already a difficult and emotionally upsetting time was to try and resolve things as fairly and as equitably as possible. Neither of us had a desire to seek reparations from the other and our only interest was to see our mutual finances dissolved in a manner that was fair and equitable. We had a house with a mortgage held in both our names that had a small amount of equity in it, some debt, and a couple of cars. As I recall looking back on it now we managed the disbursement of these things relatively simply and quickly since at the time the property market was burgeoning. We took the decision that when the property sold, the proceeds would be split to allow each of us a deposit for a rental property and the remaining equity would remain set aside until we were in a better position to move forwards with a property purchase that would benefit the kids. Debt was split between us, not equally since I had at that time an income (or at least an earning potential) significantly greater than Jo's. In our 7 or so years together I had been advancing my career in IT whilst she was for the most part focussed on being a full-time mother and just at the outset of her career in the NHS. Therefore, we felt that the fairest way to split things was for me to take on largest share of our mutual debt.

The remainder of financial consideration was directed by our working situations. Once I secured my job in Somerset and Jo had escalated her hours to full-time, we took an open and honest look at our individual finances (note, I do not refer to it as 'mutual' since from this point forwards we were separated and hence living as individuals – an important distinction to make), to determine what level of financial support I could afford to provide Jo on the basis that I was now earning 50% more than her, and she was responsible for the kids for approximately 24 days a month with me having them for the remaining 6. A monthly contribution was agreed, and a review period also. We didn't assume that it would be set in place and lived with forever more. Life went on.

Stage 2 – When we decided upon shared-parenting. By this time 18 months had passed and we had reached the conclusion that Shared-Parenting was the way forwards. Jo had advanced in her career such that her earnings were greater, but the job I had taken to move back to Manchester had also led to an increase in my earnings and so we were in a better position to mutually agree a revision to our arrangement. The challenges that I faced in adapting for the first time to being a 'proper' single parent were such that we felt we needed a new, more flexible and involved child-care facility and so employed the services of a child-minder. Following another open and honest review of our *individual* finances, we concluded that the equitable way of funding this would be for me to pick up the costs of this to offset the difference between our earnings, however I would cease to make direct contributions to Jo on a monthly basis.

Here, I feel it necessary to make an important distinction; I believe that in the course of agreeing the financial terms of your shared-parenting arrangement, whilst money may change hands on a regular basis between the two separated partners to meet various costs associated with the kids, it is very important that these are treated as separate from any financial arrangement that may exist in relation to the dissolution of the marriage (e.g. one partner paying the other a regular sum to pay off a mutual loan, or in compensation for equity in a former joint home). The notional separation of finances that are related to the relationship, from the meeting of costs as part of the shared-parenting arrangement is necessary to truly embrace the Golden Rules of shared-parenting.

If the sense of doing the right things for the kids is to pervade, for you both to do whatever is best for them and to feel, quite rightly, proud of yourselves that the kids' needs are being prioritised over and above the other aspects of dissolution of the relationship, then this is really the only way things can move forwards.

This approach is necessary both at the outset of the agreement and at all points when this is reviewed. It will require regular review and monitoring as life moves on, each person moves on in their career, perhaps re-marries, and certainly as the kids get older and the expenses change (from child-care costs, on to the cost of sports clubs, mobile phone bills, the latest trainers, school trips and beyond).

Here, I present my step-by-step plan, for agreeing the finances of the shared-parenting arrangement:

1) Agree the financial terms of your separation (home equity, debt, investments and so-on) separately from the financial terms of your shared-parenting arrangement, and always maintain this separation conceptually, even if sums of money change hands in relation to both on a regular basis.

2) Discuss the terms of your shared-parenting as openly as you can, giving your ex as much visibility of your costs and income as you feel comfortable, at least at the outset. It will ensure that the distribution of child-related costs is understood and appreciated by both parties and that the arrangement reached is fair.

3) Review your arrangement regularly, if not 6-monthly, then annually, and certainly at important 'life-events' (such as at the changing of jobs, when one or other of you perhaps enters into a new relationship). Accept that child-related expenses will change as they get older, and treat these changes as means of adapting your arrangement.

4) Treat any money that you pay out to your ex as being targeted at the particular child-related expense rather than merely a contribution into their current account. It feels better to know that, for example, you each meet the costs of your kids during the weeks they are with you, but that you pay for their after-school child-care, rather than feeling resentful when your ex turns up in a new car when you have been paying £300 a month into the shared-parenting arrangement. *Maintain and embrace this distinction.*

5) Maintain open and honest communication. It doesn't have to be that you are constantly telling your ex about every penny that you have spent, and I would actively discourage you from doing so, since it erodes the sense of applying Golden Rule #1. However, if you have paid for a school trip, mention it to your ex. If they have paid for a sports club subscription for a term, expect them to mention it. Be mindful of the overall spread of expense between the kids' two homes since you would like your ex to be doing the same, right?

6) Where possible, strive for the point at which you cease to have an on-going financial element to your shared-parenting arrangement that is explicitly stated, but instead you each meet the costs of your kids during the weeks that they are with you, and that the general sense is that they are supported equally by both of you. There will always be things that come up (school Ski Trips and the provision of a mobile phone are two recent examples in my family) that will demand a quick discussion as to who will foot the bill, or how this will be split. The more accustomed you become to discussing such matters, the quicker and easier these things get handled.

I could go on, and outline the minutiae of detail regarding these guidelines and how we have agreed upon the distribution of costs. However, I feel that the most important thing to take from this section of the book is that this potentially complex part of the dissolution of a relationship can impinge upon the success of a shared-parenting arrangement if it is not treated as separate to the financing of your kids' lives. What I hope the above illustrates is that this contention can be minimised if you employ some relatively simple principles in your discussions of these matters.

Golden Rule #6 –The financial terms of a shared-parenting arrangement should always be negotiated, reviewed, managed and implemented separately from any other financial arrangements associated with the dissolution of the relationship. Treat any on-going payments that are not split equally between the parents as being focussed on the kids and maintain this distinction. Review the arrangement regularly and strive for an equitable 50/50 split.

When is shared-parenting an option?

Having discussed the pre-existing conditions that must exist, how the kids' time may be split between their two homes and factors contributing to this, and the funding of the arrangement, the final question is regarding when this arrangement is viable and feasible.

I am reluctant to offer a checklist of conditions which need to be met to make this a possibility, since I think that the unfortunate, and rather unhelpful answer to the question is that *it all depends*. The things it all depends on will be driven by the kids, the individual circumstances of the family and the direction in which the family want to take things. Things that might fall into this category, but which I am not considering (and why) are summarised below

- Any specific health-care needs associated with the kids (e.g. longstanding regular hospital appointments need to be attended, specific medical treatments or equipment/adaptations that are required to the home) – such factors will undoubtedly complicate the setting up of the shared-parenting arrangement but it is assumed that both parents are equally capable and committed to meeting these needs;

- Any disabilities that the kids may have that require specific care or abilities to deal with – again, it is assumed that both parents are equally able to manage these factors;
- Any opinions that friends or extended-family may have on the setting up of shared-parenting will be disregarded if not favourable. It is assumed that both parents are committed to the idea and see the merit of it over the alternatives, to a sufficient degree as not to be swayed by negative opinions of others (more on this later)

The factors that I do wish to discuss are somewhat simpler and more obvious but still worthy of discussion.

At what age is shared-parenting advisable/a possibility for my children? – At the point at which Jo and I parted, logistics and numerous other circumstantial factors were not conducive to shared-parenting even if we had wanted to set up such an arrangement. Having reflected upon this, I strongly suspect that *in the case of my kids* this wouldn't have been an arrangement that most effectively met their needs in the first instance. It pains me to admit this as I consider myself to have played a pretty hands-on role during their early infancy. I was no stranger to the night-time change and feed whether it was a working day or not, I tried to be active in bath-time, play-time and in school-runs and playgroups alike. However, when we parted with a 5-year-old and a 2-year-old I know that the kids needed their Mum just a bit more than they needed their Dad. Had I not been as hands-on as I had been I still think that I could have risen to the challenge of meeting their needs as a single parent but as it happened I was used to doing everything for them anyway, so when they were with me this wasn't a shock. That said, I did only have to do it for about 6 days a month on my own to begin with!

It is hard to identify a point at which they actually became ready to adapt to the shared-parenting arrangement, but all I can say is when we set out on that path when my eldest was 7 and my youngest just a month off being 4, it was apparent that they were more than old enough to fit into the arrangement that had been built around them. I am reluctant to offer 4 as a milestone and it may be that it was having had the initial 18 month period to adjust to the new way of life (even though on asking, neither of them can remember this phase of their life in any great detail), that allowed them to slot into the shared-parenting arrangement when it was put in place. Nonetheless I offer this as my own personal experience. The individual kids and their respective maturity will no doubt play a part in how ready they are for it.

In conversations with other parents who have established shared-parenting arrangements for their children, it seems that there is some evidence to back up the above assertions and it will be down to the individual child's maturity and adaptability as to how well they will adopt the arrangement. Furthermore, there seems to be some consensus that around the age of 4 when most kids are likely to be in school or school-run nursery they will be starting to step out into the world in a semi-independent way. Such milestones no doubt contribute to a child's ability to adapt to the outside world, for even the clingiest of children so it is probably no surprise that this also holds for their switching between their parents.

Other factors that could well play a part in the age from which a child is able to adopt shared-parenting may include the child's developmental level in terms of feeding; clearly a child who is breastfeeding, even if only once per day will not be able to be apart from Mum. Similarly twins (or triplets, or quads and so on) could offer a particular challenge for one or other parent to manage on their own and splits involving such scenarios may well be catered for in extended family moving in with one or other parent to support them in the parenting in the short to medium term. Such support is not likely to be portable between the child's two homes and as such could be prohibitive to establishing a shared-parenting arrangement, for infants and young children at least.

The main factor in determining whether your kids are ready for a shared-parenting arrangement is in assessing the maturity of your child, in truly knowing them and anticipating within a little at least how they will adapt. The fact that you are reading this book suggests that you have probably been a hands-on parent who knows their child and wants to remain a significant part of their life, and as such making such a judgement should not be an insurmountable challenge.

Having discussed a few of the key criteria that I believe are necessary as a foundation to a shared-parenting arrangement I will now go on to discuss a number of the other key lessons, tips and points of learning that I have gathered in the 10+ years since we started our shared-parenting arrangement. The Golden Rules described above are doubtless of great importance, but there are several more to highlight.

Chapter 4 – Living with it

It is one thing to discuss a major undertaking at a high level. It is quite another to plan it in detail, and another yet still to put your plan in action. Having made the decision to establish a shared-parenting arrangement and having agreed between us the main aspects of the agreement, it was time to put it into practice.

In at the deep end
In common with the way in which changes had previously occurred in our lives and those of our kids, it came to pass that we entered into the shared-parenting arrangement feet first and without any kind of breaking-in period; as a wise man probably once said, "if you're going to put your foot in it, go up to the groin". This seems fairly extreme perhaps, however I think it was the right thing to do and certainly not something that we had any fears or concerns about. Apart from anything else I actually don't see that there could have been any other way of entering into the arrangement.

When we had moved on from all living in one home, to me living in the south and seeing the kids at weekends and the kids living with Jo during the week it was not something that we were able to transition into gradually; it just happened. I won't lie and say it was easy, and many were the evening phone-calls with the kids where I found myself trying to pacify them (well, mainly the eldest one) as to why we couldn't "all live together anymore in the old house" or explaining why I was so far away. Equally there were the numerous obligatory calls where things had all gone awry in Manchester with the kids and the first I was aware of it was when I was phoned to attempt to calm a fraught and angst-ridden child due to some event or another. I think we would have been foolish to expect that things would have unfolded in any other way. As much as the main thrust of this book is upon the positive aspects of shared-parenting it would be unrealistic to ignore that since this is fundamentally about the breakdown of families, there is inevitably a certain amount of pain and hurt that comes part and parcel within the subject no matter how much of a success you attempt to make of things.

Whilst we had no choice in the new arrangements being established quickly, I believe it was also a good thing in allowing us all to get on and adapt to the new way that things were. As a parent it is extremely painful to know that your kids are hurting and struggling to adapt to the way their lives are. No doubt the parting of their parents must be one of the most painful things that the average child from any background has to contemplate. There is undoubtedly an inherent desire on the part of the parents to want to make this as pain-free a process as possible when it has to happen and it was this instinct that must have just kicked-in for me and made the events of the following months happen and be managed as best as I could.

Whilst I am keen to avoid portraying myself as someone who lacks consideration or empathy, I am a firm believer in doing things as quickly as possible rather than procrastinating or drawing them out. I believe in doing everything I can to make change acceptable to all those involved and to tackle the worst first and get it over with. I rip the sticking plaster off swiftly. I clean the toilet first when doing the housework. As a kid I always did my homework before going out to play. That's just who I am. I could probably write a book on this approach itself and it would be called something along the lines of Just Do It (if I wasn't fearful of reprisals from a certain athletics-goods company). When you know that something is unpleasant or has the potential to be unpleasant, but you know that sooner or later you're going to have to go through it, I see very little point in putting it off. Without wishing to labour the point, I think that in the instance of making changes to the parenting arrangements of one's kids there really is no better way of implementing changes than of planning it and then doing what you intend to do for the long-term, right from the outset.

I appreciate that your individual circumstances and the needs of your child may divert you from this approach, however I suggest my approach here with strong conviction since I believe in it and have observed the experiences of others to corroborate this belief, that the option of doing the opposite does little more than draw out the inevitable outcome and prolongs the pain for the children.

To a large extent this thinking extends to any changes in a kid's life. In the context of establishing shared-parenting, let us consider a theoretical example of what would be the alternative means of achieving the same end.

Instead of being with both parents full time, the children start out with one or other parent (based on convention, this would usually be Mum) either at what used to be the shared family home, or in a new home. The other parent (in this case Dad) moves into a new home and as a means of getting the kids used to the new arrangement and the new home on a gradual basis, it is decided that this will be done incrementally. Rather than leaping into the alternate week's shared-parenting arrangement that has been discussed, it is agreed instead that the kids will stay with Mum from Monday to Friday, with Dad for weekends and then the occasional mid-week night until some point in the future when the full 50/50 split is implemented.

On the face of it, the above would seem like a viable 'softly-softly' approach to getting the kids used to things. However, in my personal view it is likely to be counterproductive. Let us look at the pros and cons:

Pros:

- The kids get time to get used to their new home.

- The kids have a period of time to adapt to being with one or other of the parents on an on-going basis.

The subtext that I think comes alongside these benefits (and I have focussed on the benefits for the kids, in line with Golden Rule #1) is the flipside that any benefit that is attained through this course of action is somewhat artificial and potentially corrosive to the benefit of what can be attained. This may be illustrated through looking at the Cons of the situation.

Cons:

- The kids maintain a reliance on, and a view of their old family home as their main place of residence. An important distinction to make for the parents at least is that neither one home must be considered as the 'main' place of residence. The kids may end up referring to Mum's house as home and Dad's house as 'Dad's', but it is important for Mum and Dad to encourage the view that home is where the kids are at any point in time (either Mum's or Dad's). This is particularly pertinent when Mum is staying in the former family home and this could significantly impact on the kids bonding with their new home if it doesn't have perceived equal status. Indeed their potential excitement about a new home (for experience shows that even in sad circumstances, kids can find excitement in such things) may be tempered if they aren't able to enjoy this as they might through being limited in the time they can spend there.
- There is an immediate and significant change from the previous situation where Mum and Dad were a unified parenting team to a situation where Mum is the primary carer and Dad is somewhat marginalised. This could have detrimental effects on the kids' relationship with Dad and harm the

potential for him to be considered the equal parent once the shared-parenting arrangement kicks in.
- The process of adapting to being a single parent will undoubtedly be a period of some challenge for both parents, and changes that arise in this period and norms that are established in parenting style at this point in the process are potentially going to be influenced by the amount of time the kids are spending with Mum and not with Dad at this point.

I am keen not to suggest a single way of making things happen since I think that in a lot of circumstances there may be very compelling reasons why a family cannot move directly into a shared-parenting arrangement from the splitting of the family home (clearly this was the case in my own family, but due to circumstances rather than out of desire). However, I *am* keen to encourage what I think is the best way of taking things forwards directly. Being a big proponent of doing what you say you will do, of making bold steps to maximise benefit, and of not putting off the inevitable, I think that where possible it is sensible to make the bold step straight away and to move into a shared-parenting arrangement as soon as possible. This allows everyone to adapt to the new situation from the off, to get-to-grips with the way things are going to be, and perhaps most importantly to know that this is the one step-change that needs to be made in their family life, and once adapted to, further significant changes won't need to be made again.

> *Golden Rule* #7 –Once you have agreed to move forwards with the shared-parenting arrangement, establish it and immediately start living it (or do so as soon as it is realistically viable to). Apply the same approach to other key decisions, changes and in dealing with events that will doubtlessly occur and need to be managed throughout the arrangement. The time for action is always NOW.

For the remainder of this chapter, I will mainly focus on the period from which our shared-parenting arrangement began since in line with above I consider this to be the point at which the plan was properly put into action.

In at the deep end

I will always remember my first week of having the kids in our shared-parenting arrangement, effectively week 1 of being a 'proper' single parent back in October 2007. It was a single week that felt like it lasted about a month. With every day feeling so busy and with so many things to be done it had the peculiar effect of making time feeling extremely drawn-out. Nonetheless it felt good to be embarking into a situation that felt like it had potential to be the long-term norm. I couldn't honestly say this had ever felt the case in our previous arrangement.

I was one week into my new job and had already set the scene with my new manager that my situation as a part-time single parent was something that I was just embarking upon (more on this later). Jo and I had agreed that the simplest way of implementing our 50/50 agreement was that handover day would be a Monday, and that the kids would depart from one home for school on the Monday morning and the other parent would collect them from school on a Monday night. They would then spend the following 7 nights with that parent before going back in the other direction. We discussed at the time whether other patterns would be better such as switching over mid-week, switching over on a Friday, or any other permutation and we reserved the right to adapt this or to try another pattern if we found that this wasn't working. We have never changed it which I guess speaks volumes as to what we feel works best.

My endorsement for switching on a Monday is probably mostly about personal preference but there are a number of reasons why this works for us:

1) Having a weekend at the end of my time with the kids is always a positive thing, as it gives the opportunity for what is likely to be the most relaxing and fun-focussed part of our week together as the last thing we each remember and take into the following week. Switching on a Friday would be quite the opposite.

2) Having a full week together makes it easier (in my mind at least) to plan ahead in terms of what things the kids need to take back and forth from one home to the other (more on this later) and has become particularly relevant since my eldest daughter started high school and now has a timetable that switches around on alternate weeks. This may sound like a trite example, however she knows what school books, PE kit and materials she needs for her week at mine, and for her week at her Mum's rather than having to cater for a bit of each of her timetabled weeks.

3) It makes it easier for us to cater for Bank Holidays which predominantly fall on Mondays. Knowing that Mondays are always handover day allows us to have reached the agreement that on a bank holiday we broadly split the day in two unless by prior agreement.

4) On the weeks I haven't got the kids it suits me (Golden Rule #4) to know that I have my 'kids-free weekend' immediately prior to the kids coming back to me. This allows me one last opportunity to prioritise the things I want to do immediately before they return and to make the final preparations for their return on the Monday.

I'm not aware of any evidence to suggest that one day or another works better for changeover days and I guess that as with many aspects of shared-parenting there will be a number of considerations that are individual to your circumstance. Mondays work best for us anyway.

Setting the rules

In preparing myself and my new home for the shared-parenting arrangement it's fair to say that I was a little apprehensive about how things would work. Of course, I was used to having the kids live with me both when Jo and I were together and subsequently when they used to spend most of their weekends with me, but both of these circumstances were significantly different from the new world into which we were moving in that a) I was the sole parent in this circumstance, and b) I was now responsible for numerous other roles that weren't a part of being 'weekend parent'. Jo and I had always been resolute that we didn't want to end up in the position of one of us being the 'fun parent' and the other, the one who had to deal with the mundane, the day-to-day and the functional stuff. This was perhaps more of a danger during the period where I was distant from the kids day-to-day lives and so immediately limited in the input that I could provide into their school lives, the pastoral stuff (feeding and cleaning!) and in getting them through their day-to-day lives. I was also with them for the majority of their weekends and keen to ingratiate myself through the fun that I could have with them as a recompense for being apart from them for lengthy periods of time, both for their benefit and to appease my own guilt perhaps for being at the other end of the country from them.

In spite of these pressures though I can honestly say that during the period where I lived away I did my best to honour this pact with Jo and attempted to be as 'functional' as I could whilst also balancing the fun part of being a parent. Anyway, the point of this slight digression is to emphasize that the intention for Jo and I to be equal as authoritarian and provider of fun in equal measures for the kids was preserved as we moved into shared-parenting.

What was quite evident to me as we moved into this arrangement and which has continued to be demonstrated over time, was that there is more than one way of achieving the same results.

As a result of Jo's parenting-role when she and I first parted having been closer to that which she would fulfil in the shared-parenting arrangement, she already had her home, her rules and her way of working that would allow her to meet her needs and those of the kids'. To put it simply, I didn't.

My role in the kids' lives was quickly to broaden from what it had been at the outset of the arrangement, to include:

- Catering for the 3 of us and accommodating the dietary foibles of two kids under the age of 8
- Getting the kids to bed and up again in time for school/to go to and from the child-minders around my job
- Clothing them and keeping school uniforms, sports kit and so-on clean and ready for wear
- Caring for them through the multitude of coughs, colds, aches and pains that punctuate their lives and accommodating sick-days from school when they occurred
- Getting homework done and attending school meetings, parents evenings, assemblies and the like
- Entertaining them around school commitments

The list above could go on and on, as any parent will know if you had to compile a job-specification for the role it would be an impressively long list. The key thing for me as a person who likes structure and organisation in their life (and knowing that this works well for my kids too) was that I needed to quickly adapt to these roles that were new to me in day-to-day life if we were all going to succeed in this. Some things you just cannot prepare for and have to emerge once you are living in the situation. Others, I certainly felt that I could be prepared for.

I do not intend to compile a full list of the rules and structures that I put in place since:

a) Not everyone will be in the same circumstances nor have to cater for the same things within theirs and their kids' lives.
b) To publish a list of rules, structures and simple principles that I put in place from the outset or have added since, will no doubt portray me as a control-freak, megalomaniac or at the very least an anally-retentive weirdo, and risk turning you off reading the rest of the book. And this assertion is only partially true anyway, since I'm only a *bit* controlling... honest!

I do think though that there would be some merit in me illustrating some of the things that got me through the early days, since I feel that these demonstrate how a bit of forethought and planning of some relatively simple things in relation to our lives made the adapting to our new situation more successful and palatable.

Example - A pre-school routine/timetable – One of my 'pressure-points' in the new arrangement was my general fear over how I could get myself and the kids out of bed, cleaned, dressed, fed and watered and to our respective destinations on time, every day. Being the professional-planner that I am, I put together a simple plan, admittedly on paper but soon committed to memory that worked backwards from when I needed to leave home. I simply worked through this each day. Clearly this was the project-manager in me coming out, but don't judge me; it works! It looked something like this.

Time	Activity	Notes
06:55	Get myself up, shower, dress for work	Getting myself ready is easy, best achieved before the kids are awake
07:15	Wake the kids up, get them dressed	I found it way easier to get this done before they went downstairs, when the distractions of TV, toys, hunger and thirst become an issue. I made sure I laid out the uniforms the night before and they always bathed before bed rather than trying to get them to shower before school
07:30	Breakfast, put packed lunches in school bags and leave by the door ready to go	Simple and self explanatory. Key point to note here is that preparatory things were done the night before - making packed lunches, cleaning (or locating, then cleaning) school shoes.
07:45	Clear up after breakfast and wash dishes	I find it easier to do this as I go along, otherwise I'll feel like I'm on the back foot when I get in from work and am greeted by the breakfast dishes.
07:50	Do the girls' hair	This was no small undertaking. Two girls with long hair and a Dad with no previous history of being able to do more than a pony-tail, lead to

		some fairly sketchy plaits and pig-tail combos in the early days. There are school photos to prove it.
08:00	Leave house for the child-minders	Out the door and on our way.

There are a few key things that I hope you can take from the above (aside from the probable conclusion that if this is the level of planning that I put into one hour of our day then I'm not likely to be the most spontaneous and generally fun guy to be around):

1) I found that planning things to a reasonable level of detail ensures that we have sufficient time to do things. It also ensures that certain important things are never forgotten and pays dividends in not having to put things right or encounter unnecessary delays or distractions (e.g. making sure that we didn't forget packed lunches, or getting knocked off track by the kids refusing to co-operate while getting dressed because they were too engrossed in a TV programme).

2) Following the same pattern day-by-day quickly grooved the process for each of us making it all feel like second nature very quickly. This no doubt resulted in familiarity, acceptance and comfort, especially for the kids as they began to develop a sense of 'this is how things work here'.

3) As much as possible, I would make sure that I did things that I could the night before, such as packing lunches, getting clothes out for the following day, ensuring I'd trawled through school bags for letters that would require my attention and which were usually otherwise only remembered as we were on our way out the door on the day things were due. (As much as I've tried

to instil the responsibility for this in the kids from that point to this, it is still astonishing how many times such letters get left in bags to dissolve between sweet wrappers and library books). I maintain this approach to this day since I'd much rather know that things are organised for the next day than be assisting in a search for a pair of socks 2 minutes before we need to leave the house, but now it's their responsibility to get things organised. That this is for my benefit in feeling comfortable that things are ready is beside the point; it's for their benefit too, they just don't realise it yet!

4) If things did go wrong or we slipped off schedule, for you can never foresee all possibilities, then there was still plenty of time for us to catch up and to be honest if we were 15 minutes late leaving it wouldn't really have mattered in the scheme of things. The point is, that we (I) had a plan which would get us to where we (I) wanted to be at the time we (I) wanted us to be there, more often than not. And crucially we weren't leaving it to the last possible moment or hoping that somehow through serendipity we would get everything done on a daily basis. Also crucially for me, the above arrangement resulted in mornings that were as stress-free as they could possibly be… for the most part!

This example illustrates through a reasonably simple scenario that will apply to all single parents, that a modest amount of planning and routine can be of enormous benefit in making day-to-day life run a bit more smoothly. Such benefits are not merely constrained to making things happen quicker and easier and with more routine but I certainly believe also extend to helping everyone feel more comfortable and well-adapted to the situation all the quicker. I maintain that this was the case for me and my kids, and has continued to be the way that things work best for us all to this day although the ins and outs of the daily routine have evolved as time has gone on; there is no way my daughters would let me do their hair now, for example!

I have included below a few of the other ways in which I attempted to make life run more smoothly, mainly as high-level pointers that may or may not be of use or interest. These all come with the usual health-warning that one size will undoubtedly not fit all and that you should only consider these as examples rather than rules for success!

- I always planned what we would be having for our evening meal the following day, such that I could prepare in advance or make sure that I knew what I needed to buy from the supermarket before getting home the following day. Impromptu trips to the supermarket are undoubtedly to be avoided for the benefit of parents and kids alike.
- Food shopping would usually be done with one or two big shops a month, preferably in weeks when I didn't have the kids. This would then mean that during kids-weeks I could get fresh food on my way home from work and not have to drag them round the supermarket.
- I always insisted (and still do) on the kids going to bed at a regular time. This should be a general rule for *all* kids in my opinion but is also doubly important in a shared-parenting arrangement. I believe this is part and parcel of kids getting enough rest which positively influences all aspects of their life (health, academic ability, concentration, behaviour and so-on), and for younger kids this is also an essential part of building routine and structure into their life. I don't enforce a bed-time on myself, but I have learned that I function best with 7 to 8 hours sleep a night, and do less well if I get less sleep than this. It is an important lesson to learn for kids too. Furthermore, it is intense being a single parent, and I believe that it is essential that there is

some time at the end of the day which is ring-fenced for the parent to get their own head-space, to switch off, and to do their own thing even if this is focussed in part on getting things prepared for the next day such as making packed lunches and catching up on laundry. Getting the kids to bed in good time allows for this.

- In spite of the near 4 year age difference between my kids, I have always worked to a joint bed-time. This has caused a few disagreements over the years, but I feel it has always smoothed out more disagreements than it has contributed to. The eldest has always had the proviso of being allowed to read a book or listen to music before going to sleep, for longer than the youngest, but it has been a good part of the routine that they go off to bed at the same time. This hasn't even changed much since they've get older and I'm sure in the not too distant future I will be the first to retire for the evening, but not just yet!

The list could again continue for pages and pages, but undoubtedly some of the items on it would be considered superfluous and others more relevant. The key thing that I wanted to draw-out from my experience is this; whilst I didn't necessarily sit down at the outset and try to think about all the possible ways in which I could exert control over my children for the sake of it, I certainly went into shared-parenting knowing that I could make it work best for the kids and myself if I employed a degree of structure and planning. By taking this approach to those activities and times of day that could quickly descend into anarchy (or at the very least cause an increase in my blood-pressure) if things went awry, I felt I was giving myself and my kids the best chance of making this work.

Two homes, two different ways of doing things

Having extolled the virtues of establishing a consistent and repeatable way of doing things or getting things done, I feel it is essential to discuss one of the other most pertinent things I have learned as a parent sharing custody of my kids with my ex.

Most books that I have read on the subject of shared-parenting, or parenting when families part, will emphasize the importance of a consistent approach, consistent rules, and of trying to make the structures of life the same in both homes whether the kids are with both parents equally, or if they live predominantly with one parent and have limited visitation with the other. I completely agree with the spirit of this suggestion as I think there can be nothing more confusing or potentially disruptive for a child than knowing how to adapt to two completely different world-orders. However, I think that the suggestion needs to be caveated such that this commonality is confined to the overall approach taken to parenting, the emphasis that is placed on key aspects of a child's upbringing (such as the importance of manners, the role of family, perspective on culture and society, the degree of aspiration with which a child is brought up, the importance of education and so-on). What I think is largely irrelevant to the lives of kids in terms of consistency is the smaller things, the ins-and-outs of the day-to-day, the little stuff that is really quite irrelevant in the wider scheme of things. On the face of it this may seem to contradict what I have said previously in that I have placed enormous emphasis on relatively small stuff above (such as whether breakfast dishes are washed before school, or whether both kids go to bed at the same time in spite of age). What I mean is exemplified as follows;

In my house, the kids go to bed at a consistent time each night. Before I go to bed, I know that their uniforms are out and ready for them to put on in the morning.

Their lunches are packed and in the fridge, ready to be taken out. Their homework is done and their shoes are probably clean and by the front door; they are certainly in a pair. The next morning they will probably be woken up by me before they are ready to and all things being equal, will probably be sat, ready and waiting to go with at least 5 minutes to spare before we leave the house. They will invariably be at school early.

In their Mum's house the kids will probably be in bed within a window of plus or minus 30 minutes from the previous night. Their lunches may or may not be packed the night before and they may end up having to pop to the convenience shop round the corner before school the next day to pick up a piece of fruit or a juice box for their lunch since these may have run out. Their uniforms and shoes will be where they took them off. Their homework is done. The next morning they get up when they wake each other up, and in a whirlwind of chaos get themselves ready as they gradually do what needs to be done before leaving. Their Mum will take them to school when they are ready, and they are always at school on time, seldom all that early.

The point of the two illustrations above is to show that although the two scenarios above are vastly different, the key overarching principles are the same and the important stuff is the same in each scenario. Regardless of which home they are at in any given week, the kids get to school on-time each day, fully equipped, with their lunches to sustain them through the day and with homework having been done.

It is no surprise that the two situations are completely different since Jo and I are completely different people and I would challenge that most people reading this will acknowledge the same point regarding their ex. It was not a source of contention when we were together and nor is it now, it's just a fact. Generally speaking I like things to be structured and ordered and will put myself (and others) out in a bid to make things so. Jo is able to function in a more chaotic world and adopts a more laissez-faire approach to life. If things can be done in advance to aid a smoother life, I will do them. Jo doesn't stress about such things and trusts that they will get done when they need to be done, by whoever needs to do them. I get comfort in myself knowing that I am pre-empting future stress and hassle, whereas Jo feels comfortable going with the flow. The point though is that we both have the same aspirations, goals, beliefs and hopes for our kids, and that hasn't changed just because we split up. In this scenario we both want our kids to get to school on time each day, well rested, equipped for the rigours of the day, and with the underlying security of knowing that they are loved. That isn't affected by whether their lunch is packed the night before or 10 minutes before they leave for school.

This used to be something that I struggled with immensely and I think that my feelings, whilst coming from the right place (motivated by wanting the best for the kids) were misguided in the extreme. I would on occasion hear snippets from the kids over 'the way things work at Mums' and would feel frustrated that the same structure and approach that I employed in day-to-day life wasn't followed at her house. I mean, surely it must have been evident to her that everything ran harmoniously and smoothly in my house?!?

Notwithstanding the fact that each person will have their own views on what is the best way of running a home (and I fully expect that many will sympathise with and relate to Jo's way over mine) the reality is that because Jo and I had got the overarching principles right, it simply didn't matter. In this case the devil simply was not in the detail.

This was all illustrated to me in very plain terms in a valuable and enlightening demonstration that occurred only a few years ago. On this occasion I had cause to be at Jo's house early one morning to see the kids into school one Monday morning, since Jo had to leave her home at 7am and it happened to be convenient for me to see the girls to school on that day rather than her making an alternative arrangement for them to stay elsewhere (flexible-rigidity in action!). The circumstances are anyway rather irrelevant, the point is I was there to get the girls to school and without having thought about it too much, I guess I arrived envisaging that I would be following my routine in her house.

With this intention in mind you might guess that my frustration level began to rise pretty quickly as I spotted the packed lunch boxes still full with last Friday's cling-film and apple cores on the kitchen surface (lunches not made), uniforms strewn across the landing, just one school shoe on the hall floor, its pair nowhere to be seen. And then it happened…

The girls emerged from their bedroom having just woken up. Initial surprise to see me rather than their Mum was replaced by acceptance as they then remembered the arrangement that was in place for the day. They proceeded with efficiency and purpose that I have never observed in them before, to co-operatively and methodically get on with the task of each preparing their breakfast, making their packed lunches and then getting themselves ready for school without so much as a word or request from me to do so along the way. They even made me a cup of tea without me asking!

Now I'm sure that to many this is not such a massive undertaking or significant an achievement on their parts, and I agree that for kids of 8 and 12 (as they were at the time) to be getting themselves ready for school isn't all that big a deal. However, what was shocking was the stark comparison between what they would normally do at my house (where I essentially had to initiate the activity and encourage and cajole them through the entire process from getting out of bed to getting out of the front door, whilst presenting them with their breakfasts and packed-lunches along the way) compared to what they were doing *by instinct* here at their Mum's house.

The obvious point to make from this example is that clearly the norms associated with the pre-school breakfast routine at their Mums were completely ingrained in them in the same way that the norms for the same routine at my house were equally ingrained. The key factor it seems is about where they are! At Mum's house, Mum's rules apply and work perfectly well thank you. At Dad's, we do what works at Dad's.

There were a number of things that I took from this experience:

- It is okay for the way-of-life to be completely different (in terms of the little details) at each home. The same results can be achieved by different means and the only thing that really matters is whether the rules work *in that environment* for the kids;
- Kids are massively adaptable when it comes to doing things in a certain way at each home, and in recognising and respecting different sets of rules, as long as the consistency of purpose is there throughout;
- If the kids feel like each of their parents has a reason for things being a certain way then they will respect that and work within it provided that the parents respect each other's rules too. I am not aware of Jo being critical of how I get things done (although I would suspect that she would raise an eyebrow at how much structure I like to have in place, just as I do regarding what I have observed about her way of doing things) and I don't criticise her

for doing things her way. The bottom line is that I may not agree with her way but it works for her and more importantly the kids when they are with her. As such I respect her rules but equally don't feel pressured to adapt mine to fit with hers.

- Kids will adapt to two completely different 'world-orders' without even thinking about it. It is okay to try and micro-analyse and adapt the way that you want life to run in your home and how this contrasts with life at the other parent's home; the main thing is to be happy with how you run things (being mindful of the Golden Rules at all time) and the rest will follow.

This final point was emphasized to me a mere 24 hours later when back at my house for a week, I found myself having to cajole them through the morning routine, as usual!

> *Golden Rule #8* – It is advisable to think about a structured way of doing things, to help adapt to and maintain the shared-parenting arrangement, in as much or as little detail as you feel appropriate to yours and your kids' needs. Expect though that your structures and rules may be different from those of your ex, and don't feel pressured to adapt to their way of working. The key thing is that your overall goals, beliefs, aspirations and priorities for your kids are aligned which will ensure that your kids have a consistent parenting experience across both homes.

In the above I have attempted to outline some of the fundamental things that were addressed at the outset of the shared-parenting arrangement, since these were things that I believe with hindsight were good to have set out from the beginning.

Within the following chapters I also hope to draw out some equally valid and valuable learning points.

Chapter 5 – A united front

Much of this book so far has focussed upon the steps associated with establishing a shared-parenting arrangement in the context of how to manage the individual home, or your half of the arrangement. One of the key facets or critical success factors in making the arrangement work however, is in managing the delicate balance that is in acknowledging that the parents of this family are no longer together in a marriage or partnership but are still united as parents to the kids. As you can probably foresee, this is one of the most challenging aspects of the arrangement since it is one that requires the typically emotionally challenging and charged aspects of the split to have to be revisited to some degree.

The key premise behind the united front is to acknowledge the fact that whilst Mum and Dad are no longer together in a relationship or marriage, their shared interest as parents to the kids remains. Adopting this approach demonstrates a number of things:

To the kids:

- Mum and Dad still respect each other and can remain friendly or at least civil towards each other in spite of not being in love any more (whether kids understand or appreciate the nuances of this at a young age or not, eventually they will realise the importance of it);
- In spite of their differences Mum and Dad are able to focus on the needs of the kids first and foremost, respecting each other enough to entrust each other with the sole care of their kids on an equal basis;
- That whilst there may be other aspects of life that they disagree on, when it comes to parenting, rules and decisions made on the basis of their kids, they

are united and share a purpose and demonstrate unity in regard to those decisions;

To each other:

- Regardless of what caused the split and who was responsible for splitting (if indeed either was to blame) it demonstrates that the happiness of their kids can be put to the fore and differences put aside;
- It demonstrates that issues and factors pertinent to the failed relationship may be separated from the business of being parents to the children. It is not essential for the biological parents of the children to be together in a relationship in order to give their children the best upbringing possible.

To the 'outside world':

- I am not generally prone to being overly concerned about what anyone else thinks about my personal circumstances or those pertaining to my family and children in particular. However, based on personal experience and things that the majority of people have told me it seems that the general perception is that an arrangement that is primarily focussed about doing the right thing for the sake of the kids and putting the adults' differences aside is considered both admirable and progressive in its outlook. The establishment of shared-parenting and of maintaining regular contact with my kids whilst also playing a significant part in their lives is something of which I am extremely proud.
- It shows that the parents are not interested in 'scoring points' off of each other, or in trying to establish themselves in particular roles (the fun one, the authoritarian and so-on) but rather that they approach joint decisions regarding the kids with a mutual focus, a unified approach and determination

to do the right thing for the kids rather than being motivated by any other minor gain (for example over each other). For example, we always made a point to go together to parents evenings at schools and similar events, present as the joint-parents of our children if not as a married couple.

There are numerous benefits to be gained from taking this approach provided that it can be established in the right way with the correct motivators in the first place. There are a number of things that may need to be dealt with effectively by the parents in order to make this a real possibility.

First and foremost, in ensuring that Golden Rule #1 is satisfied at all times it may often arise that one or other of the parents is forced into a position of compromise in relation to a particular decision, piece of guidance or action in relation to the kids that is not exactly what they would like to be made, given or taken in their view of an ideal world. A simple example of this would be my personal preference that the kids do their homework in the evenings after school to allow us all to have our free-time at the weekend (in much the same way as I did as a kid). Jo's preference may be that the kids are given autonomy to decide when they do homework. We are both motivated by wanting the kids to realise that homework is a priority; I want them to learn the value of getting done what you have to do over what you would like to do, whereas Jo wants them to learn that it is necessary to prioritise things in your life to ensure that they all get done. I believe that these are both valid lessons and can talk to the kids about my approach just as Jo can about hers. The unified approach in our joint-parenting is that the kids know that completing their homework on time is a priority and that we will neither of us be happy should this slip.

Golden Rule #9 – Whilst both parents are unlikely to agree on all matters that require a united-front of parenting, the key thing is to agree on the over-arching principles that shape your shared-parenting arrangement. Within this, matters such as expectations for the kids' behaviour, your aspirations and goals for them, the freedoms and disciplines you want them to grow-up with and the priorities for their upbringing should be understood and agreed upon by you both.

There will always be difficult decisions that need to be reached mutually, such as disciplinary matters in relation to things that happen when the kids are at one or other home. On numerous occasions I have been called upon by Jo to reinforce a punishment that she has applied or a judgement that she has reached without me having been previously aware of the circumstances that led to it. An example of this would be grounding or loss of privileges for a period of time spanning the kids' transit between our homes for the misuse of the internet. Whilst the offence occurred while the kids were with their Mum the punishment will span both homes for a period of time and it is essential that this is uniformly applied across the homes. Equally important is that the circumstances that led to the punishment are understood by all so that the lesson can sink in for the child. The discussion of the issue and unified application of the punishment are essential to ensure that the circumstances of the offence and the meting out of the punishment don't get distorted or undermined.

Similarly you will find in the course of shared-parenting that joint discussions are required on numerous other matters that aren't about the enforcing of rules or the application of punishments, but that are related to the decisions that need to be taken on subjects that crop up in the child's day-to-day life. Such decisions vary in significance and size and one topic area that seems repeatedly to require decisions to be made on numerous matters is in relation to education (which school the kids will be sent to, extra-curricular classes and sports that a child will take part in, options that will ultimately be taken when the child studies for formal qualifications, whether a child will take part in residential school trips and how these will be funded, whether the child will take music lessons in/out of school; the list goes on and on). Similarly there could be decisions relating to:

- the child's health (who is responsible for ensuring the child gets inoculations, sight and hearing tests, attending doctors, dentists and hospital appointments and so-on)
- leisure time (which sports are pursued, whether they take part in cubs or brownies, attend regular religious ceremonies)
- in relation to the on-going clothing and self-expression of the child (otherwise known as 'they can't go out looking like that'!).

There is a vast myriad of different discussions that would need to be had at any given time relating to an enormous range of subjects. Your challenge as the parents in the shared-parenting arrangement is in managing these.

I believe the balance is in establishing a means of communication between Mum and Dad that ensures that the really important stuff is considered seriously with proper unimpeded conversation that focuses on the issue at hand. Conversely though there needs to be a recognition that in shared-parenting each of Mum and Dad has undertaken to empower each other with sole parenting of the kids for periods of time and hence a certain amount of decision-making autonomy needs to be entrusted by each other, to each other so that the minor decisions and more trivial matters are dealt with individually in line with the overarching principles of the shared-parenting agreement. After all, we should not lose sight of the fact that

Mum and Dad are no longer together in a relationship, and would not necessarily wish to be flung together in a regular dialogue on every little decision that needed to be taken, any more than they would tackle such things consultatively if they were still married.

An effective means of considering situations and discussing and making agreements is demonstrated by that which has evolved between me and Jo, the guiding principles of which I have outlined below:

1) We entrust each other with the small, day-to-day decisions and rely on each other to inform each other where these will impact on the other, or where there needs to be some logistical arrangement made between us or a potential financial settlement/consideration may be required. Examples of things that fall in this category would be:
    a. Me signing one of the kids up for a school day trip and sending the money into school where the trip fell in a week when the kids were due to be with Jo.
    b. Jo signing one of the kids up for a term of tennis lessons (we agree that the kids should be encouraged to pursue as much sport as they are willing to, and we mutually fund these things) where the lessons occur weekly hence when the kids are at either home.

Such things will usually be notified to the other by text or email or in passing conversation.

2) Some things would be considered of moderate significance (if not urgency) and may require our joint input in terms of making arrangements, either because we both could reasonably have an opinion or an interest in the outcome. In these instances, we would usually discuss these in passing when

the girls are passing back and forth between us (e.g. when dropping the girls' belongings off on changeover day). Examples may include:

   a. Arrangements for the kids care during a school half-term holiday
   b. Plans for where the kids will be going for family holidays, and with whom

We don't go as far as getting an agenda together for such things, but it is often useful to drop a text message to each other as an aide-memoire ("when I see you remind me to mention plans for half term" or something similar usually does the trick)

3) Where there are things of greater significance we make sure that we allocate some time where we can sit down and discuss them properly either in person (preferably) or over the phone, but certainly without having to discuss them in front of the kids and without any time pressure to get things resolved in a short period of time. Examples of this kind of discussion would include:

   a. Concerns over elements of schooling such as whether progress at school is satisfactory
   b. Issues around the child's happiness/personal difficulties (such as bullying)
   c. Key decisions such as which secondary school to apply to

These discussions don't need to be managed as a formal meeting but the key thing is to allow for appropriate space for the discussion to be held, and adequate time for things to be considered properly and without the input/interruption of the kids (until this is appropriate).

I suggest that the above three-tiered model for decision and discussion works well for most things that occur day-to-day in a shared-parenting arrangement. Again though, it is based on my experience and is offered only as a guide or illustrative model. The key thing is to figure out a model that works for you and then ensure that you both use it!

> *Golden Rule #10* – Where possible, agree on an approach to presenting a united front that ensures a level of trust and autonomy is given by Mum and Dad to each other to deal with the day-to-day in line with the overarching principles of the shared-parenting arrangement. In addition to this, ensure that you both agree with and understand the means by which you will handle the more serious or complex matters and ensure that you devote adequate time to this process.

The examples above illustrate the complete reliance on there being good communications between Mum and Dad for the purposes of negotiating and discussing things that come up, and demonstrating a unified approach in how rules are enforced and decisions taken; this is also essential to maintaining the shared-parenting arrangement as a whole and will be a theme that I come back to time and again.

United in the good stuff

The above discussion points and examples are largely focussed on the application of rules and the enforcement of punishments and the serious stuff, but the same principles can be also be applied to the giving of praise and rewards and also to things such as the giving of birthday gifts, and presents for school reports and so-on. It could even apply to things as random as the scale of payment made by the tooth fairy between two houses! (This is something that has plagued me since the day the tooth fairy showed uncharacteristic generosity when a tooth was lost at my house, and set the precedent for the scale of rewards that has cost me dearly since!). Some of these examples warrant a little further discussion.

Birthday and Christmas Gifts – This is an area that has huge potential to cause an imbalance in the shared-parenting arrangement in any instance where a lack of a unified front influences the way that gifts for the kids are bought and given by one or other parent or even by extended family on one or other side. The obvious potential source of problems is where one or other parent becomes the one who wins plaudits or favour with the kids through the giving of extravagant presents (whether they can afford it or not), or is the one who is always seen to be the provider of treats/larger sums of pocket-money and so-on. This is not to say that I believe that children should be denied the presents they wish for (within reason) but there should be a collaborative approach between the parents who are sharing the parenting responsibility such that there is a balance around what the kids receive and which parents are credited with the giving!

As with many facets of shared-parenting there is no one-way of doing things. I hope that the two methods that we've employed since we started shared-parenting are illustrative of the best ways of managing this.

> *Approach 1* - Where appropriate, the parents still buy presents jointly for the kids, deciding jointly what will be given to them, how it will be paid for (either equally or split another way that is mutually agreeable) and the gift is given to the child as a present from Mum and Dad collectively.
>
> The benefits of this kind of arrangement are that the child will presumably feel gratitude to both parents equally for the gift. Similarly, it ensures a level

of co-ordination and is a more obvious positive demonstration of the united front.

The drawbacks or rather, the complications of this arrangement that have emerged in this scenario for our family warrant a bit of discussion. The arrangement worked really well for us in the first instance for the reasons outlined above. Similarly, in the early years after our split we undertook to spend the kids' birthdays and part or all of Christmas day (the two key gift-giving seasons in our family) together, if not as a family in the traditional sense, then at least with both Mum and Dad present for part of the day (more on this later). However, as time has gone on and the kids are older and comfortable with the shared-parenting arrangement we have moved to a situation where we alternate who the kids spend Christmas and occasionally their birthdays with. This immediately starts to reduce the appeal of joint gift-giving since it may logistically prevent both parents from being there when the joint-gift is given and opened; surely one of the best parts of giving gifts in seeing the response it gets!

The other pertinent factor to this area is the potential changes when either Mum or Dad moves on in life and enters into a new partnership or even re-marries. This is a complex area that will be discussed in its own right later on, but I mention it now since in this circumstance it would be reasonable to expect that Mum and partner, or Dad and partner would wish to jointly give a gift to the child as being solely from them. Shared-parenting may well continue in this circumstance but just as there is benefit to the unified approach of shared-parenting, so there is also benefit to be attained from the clarity that Mum and Dad have moved on in life and have new relationships. As such, the receiving of gifts from Mum and partner separately from Dad and partner is an important indicator and feature of moving forwards in this way.

Finally, it is not to say that in this circumstance joint-presents from Mum and Dad cannot still be given to kids and we have continued to do so for more expensive items (such as a laptop to support studies when our eldest started at high school; a gift too expensive for either of us to fund individually).

Approach 2 – On the basis of the above you can probably foresee the alternative. Our other approach which has maintained the spirit of communication, fairness and parity between the two homes is to ensure that in the run up to Christmas and Birthdays we discuss and collaborate on what we (and our extended families) are intending to buy for the kids. This ensures that we are co-ordinated, do not duplicate, can ensure that our gifts are in some cases complimentary to each other and also that neither of us (or our families) unknowingly out-do each other with the gifts that are given. It also ensures that the kids receive gifts in both homes on Birthdays and Christmas (without being spoilt or getting too much so as to negate their gratitude). This approach has worked better for our kids, especially as they have grown older since it also contributes to their sense of acknowledgement that they have two homes, and parents who are not together, but they know that we are co-ordinated in what we get for them such that on occasion when they've requested something particularly expensive then they are willing to suggest that maybe we could club-together and get them it, at which point it becomes their choice; something that we are also keen to encourage as they get older.

The discussion above is broadly applicable to most elements of gift-giving for kids, but I have included a couple of other more specific examples that may be of use or interest

One-off purchases (e.g. Bikes) – We apply a similar approach to such things as we do for present buying which is to take an approach that we are mutually contributing to such purchases and that they are not something that one or other parent is due the gratitude or plaudits for. In real terms this equates to a discussion (communication being key) around what we will buy, how much each will contribute and so-on. In relation to a recent purchase of bikes for the kids since they'd both long outgrown theirs, we decided to each buy one of the bikes for them and agreed an upper price ceiling for each bike. As far as the kids were concerned they had been provided with a new bike by Mum and Dad and we each felt like the financing of this was fairly split between us.

Rewards for School Reports – I firmly believe that such things are completely discretionary and down to the individual parent to apply rather than taking a uniform approach. This is another of the areas in which we have agreed the overall principle of wanting to reward and incentivise academic achievement, but have different ways of doing this. Jo seems to favour a one-off reward or treat for a good report or set of exam results, I prefer to offer an incentive through each term, based on a certain reward for each A-Grade on the termly report (with a descending scale for each lower grade). The key thing is that we both want to encourage the kids to work hard at school and one such way to do this (unfortunately, but perhaps a sign of the consumerist-times!) is through financial reward.

Allowance/Pocket Money- This has largely been free-form between the two homes for the majority of time since we established shared-parenting in as much as Jo did what she did in regard to pocket money, and I did my thing. For my part it used to be something that I really struggled with. Living as I was on an already stretched budget, I tried to stick to a small monthly allowance for the kids which I would initially try and allocate to each weekend they were with me (basically alternate weekends). This however just prolonged the seemingly endless hours that we would trawl round the local shops with them either spending all their money on the first piece of plastic rubbish they saw (to my annoyance) or lamenting the fact that they couldn't afford the slightly more expensive piece of plastic rubbish since they always spent-first and regretted later. Not natural-born savers, my kids!

I then adapted my approach so that they got the whole months allowance in one chunk, as I thought that this would make it quicker for them to get it spent and give me back at least part of my second weekend with them in the month since they could hardly make it last past the first weekend. This worked, however I made trouble for myself in that I stipulated that they should keep the money at my house, my reasoning being that I had given it and they should use it as a diversion when they were with me. I also realized latterly that this wasn't smart either since this would prevent them from learning that if they saved money from me and that from their Mum, they could then afford bigger ticket items.

The approach employed now is that they get a monthly allowance and this goes into their wallet (one of the things that traverses from their Mum's to mine and back again) and they can spend it at will or save it. Latterly, both children on their 12th Birthdays got their first bank accounts and now get their monthly allowance paid into that by each of me and their Mum and this will be used along with our guidance to teach her about how to manage a bank account.

The key thing is that it is down to the individual parents to give as much or as little pocket money to their kids as they see fit. I also personally link this to activities such as keeping their bedrooms tidy and other basic household chores as well as keeping school work up to standard. Similarly, I hope that paying them at a set point each month and then not giving them more money until next 'payday' will give them an early view of life in the real world and a need to budget. All aspirations (perhaps unrealistic) at this point, but who knows!

What I hope you take from the above examples is that the key aspect with taking a unified approach in your shared-parenting whether it be how much to spend on a Christmas gift, how to punish a child for watching music videos on YouTube when they should be researching the Roman empire, or what time your kids should go to bed is that communication between you and the other parent of your child is key. No matter what structure you put in place to enable this communication and whether it is formal or informal, over the phone, text, email or in person, regular or ad-hoc, that it is vital that you and your ex communicate regularly and effectively *on matters relating to your kids* to assure the success of your shared-parenting agreement.

> ***Golden Rule #11*** – Communication between you and your ex is CRITICAL to the successful maintenance of your shared-parenting. Ensure that you are able to discuss matters in a manner and with due consideration, time and sensitivity depending on the issue at hand.

This is perhaps the second most important of the Golden Rules.

Chapter 6 – Logistics

I want to discuss the logistics associated with shared-parenting since I feel it is something that whilst on the face of it a relatively minor part of the arrangement, is something that brings about its own challenges. Once we established shared-parenting in 2007 with the kids' two homes merely a mile or so apart, there were not too many challenges caused in getting them back and forth between the houses or the places where they would wish to go. Within this chapter I have included within some pointers around occurrences to do with place and where the kids are, have been or are going to since these are still factors worthy of consideration. All will become clear.

Home is where I hang my hat
As I have stated already, our intention at the outset of the shared-parenting arrangement was always that the kids should have two homes, not that either Mum's or Dad's would be perceived as their main place of residence but rather that both should feel like home. A friend of mine once said to me that he never liked to feel temporary about where he lived and this is something that really stuck with me and which I have always applied in my own life. As someone who has moved home a fair amount, and worked in jobs where I was often required to stay in hotels during the working week for extended periods of time, I am unfortunately accustomed to feeling the lack of certainty and familiarity that stems from not having your possessions around you, of not feeling the familiar pillow beneath your head when you lay down to go to sleep, and of not generally feeling at home. It has always been of great importance to me that the kids have felt that within the obvious constraint of only being here 50% of the time, that nonetheless my home is their home, *our home,* and I'm pretty sure that the same is true at their Mum's too.

The obvious means of achieving this has been through two main means. First and foremost, I have ensured that they each have their own space that is their own to decorate, organise and fill with the pictures and trinkets that children seem to want around them. A key difference between my home and Jo's has been that at mine they have separate bedrooms, and at Jo's they have shared. Paradoxically it came to light fairly early on that whilst I billed this to them as a major selling point of my house when we started with shared-parenting, thinking that every child wanted their own room, it actually turned out to be something that they weren't keen on. It seems that although they fight like cat and dog from time-to-time, they actually still like being close by each other and a shared bedroom was clearly back then, and still remains to be a source of comfort to them.

Aside from the actual physical space, I have also been keen not to place any barriers to them having pictures of Jo or their extended-family on her side in their rooms at my house. Indeed, I think it should be expected that kids would like a picture of the parent that they are not currently with, near to them and I have never discouraged this. Similarly, the extended family is really important to us and I am always in favour of there being family photos on the kids' walls, even if they are of the ex-in-laws!

The second main means of achieving a sense of home for the kids has been to limit the degree to which they have to physically 'move' between their two homes on changeover day. Obviously I don't mean the physical act of travelling but more that we have essentially negated the need for a large volume of kit, clothing and possessions to be transported from one home to the other on changeover day. The rationale behind this approach is that if we were able to achieve the position whereby the kids were effectively surrounded by familiar things in familiar surroundings in each of their homes and if they had access to the things they wanted or needed in these places then essentially the key aspects of what would make either of these places feel like home are fulfilled.

Lessons were learned along the way as regards the downsides to having to shift loads of things between the two homes. In the early days we had a large holdall that was used as the means of passing things back and forth on changeover day. Whilst the intent behind this bag was that it would only be used for the essential personal items and a subset of their clothing, it quickly became apparent that things were being shoved in the bag and left for weeks on end since they were simply not essential either to the kids or to us. Furthermore, its very presence was illustrative of the kids being 'on-the-move' when they travelled between their homes which was against the ethos that we were trying to promote. A final detractor from this approach was that at that time, the kids were being dropped off before school at the child-minder's and picked up by the other parent from there after work on changeover day which meant that the bag was being left at her house, much to her annoyance. This was the final (small) straw that broke the back of the (albeit rather inconsequential) camel and from this point on we resolved that we wouldn't continue to routinely ship the kids back and forth with a large bag of their things just for the sake of it.

Skipping ahead to the practical steps that we have taken to make this work I have outlined below some of the main things that we employ to keep things ticking over:

- As a general rule, we only own between us one set of the things that we absolutely only need one of (school uniforms, winter coats, specialist sports kit such as Karate Suits and items of greater value such as personal games consoles, MP3 players and so-on). These are the essential items that the kids take back and forth between homes and this is fairly simple to achieve. School related items will usually be with the kids since they switch over on changeover day after school and the other bits and pieces usually fit in a small rucksack that the kids either share or a small bag that each of them are encouraged to use to keep all their essentials in (a hand-bag or personal holdall that most adults use these days anyway). This bag is then collected or dropped off on changeover day.

- The kids have a full set of clothing including underwear through to outerwear and casual clothes that remain at each home. You may contend that this is an unnecessary expense but my response would be that they're only with me 50% of the time so I only need half as much of it!
- The kids are encouraged at the end of a week with either Jo or I to think about what they might need or want of their possessions in the following week and if possible these are then packed in their personal bag.
- We have duplicate chargers for mobile phones, personal games consoles, MP3 players and the like at both homes since experience has shown that these are quickly the first things that are needed, and the last things to be packed, as well as the item most likely to go missing between the two addresses.
- Where there are school letters or printed information that needs to be passed between the two homes, we encourage the kids to take this in school bags as a means of fostering responsibility on their part. If it is particularly sensitive or important we will take responsibility for handing it to each other.
- We have also arranged with school that they send duplicate letters, reports and the like to each home. This is apparently quite a common request and something that most schools should be more than capable of accommodating.

The above summarises the key principles we have adopted and whilst these things are not rocket-science (in common with many such lists included in this book) I believe they demonstrate that a little bit of forethought and consideration of the basics, and getting such things right can make life a whole lot easier and smooth-running in the execution; this means that the kids and the parents can get on with the business of living.

Golden Rule #12 – Both of your children's places of residence should feel like and be treated as their homes. This sense should come about through both places being physically decorated to feel like home, with as few of their possessions following them about as possible to encourage a sense of permanence and belonging at both homes. A few basic principles can be adopted to ensure that the transit of 'things' between homes is kept to a minimum.

There will doubtless be exceptions to the above principles, and as the years go by for me as a shared parent the learning points keep on coming. Such exceptions have included:

- For extended periods or special occasions such as school holidays or family vacations the kids have often wanted to take certain toys, possessions or items of clothing with them, or bring other things with them. Such requests are usually accommodated even if things take a few weeks thereafter to return to their rightful home. Still, no big deal; they're only things, right?
- Holiday clothes – traditionally, the kids have a couple of holidays per year, once with their Mum and extended family on her side and once with me and mine. There is little point in them having two lots of holiday clothes/beach-

wear/ski-wear and so-on, so such things are bought once and shared between the two homes

- 'Special' items of clothing seem to be becoming more of a feature for my now-teenaged elder daughter and it seems to be more of a factor to her to want to have some vital item of clothing from my house when she is at her Mum's or vice-versa. In the spirit of accommodating the whimsical life of a teenager, these requests are usually fulfilled if convenient.

I should emphasize that both Jo and I attempt to be reasonably accommodating to the kids in terms of ad-hoc requests for things that they all of a sudden need mid-week that have been left at their other home. This is also balanced with trying to encourage them to take responsibility and think about what they may need in advance, or alternatively considering whether they really need the item in question. The fact is that they didn't ask to be growing up in the shared-parenting arrangement and many of their peers will not have to contend with such a need for forward planning and having their things split between two homes (more on this concept in a bit). However, I think what is essential to note about this is that there are a couple of very valuable lessons that we are able to extract as positives from this situation to enable the kids to learn from, demonstrating that it's not simply a case of them having to make the best of a bad thing:

1) It teaches them a sense of responsibility for taking care of their things, for knowing where things are, and for thinking about what they will need to get them through the next week. In this way skills like organisation, responsibility, accountability, ownership and forward-planning are in a reasonably light and low level way, demanded of them to make their day-to-day and week-to-week lives function more easily. This is surely a valuable skill to take forward in life?

2) It enforces for them the fact that in some way 'things' are not what make the world go around and rather that it is through a sense of belonging, of being at home in an environment where you feel safe, loved and cared-for are what is really important and that the accessories, gadgets and clutter that many of us surround ourselves with in day-to-day life are not of such great significance that you cannot get by if you are parted from them for a week or so at a time.

3) It teaches them to value the things they have and to appreciate the things that really matter. A flip-side of the point above, this is often evidenced by the way that often within an hour or so of arriving at my home for a new week I will find each of them engrossed in an activity that is particular to things that live at mine. There is joy for them in the re-discovery and availability of an item that they have been apart from for a period of time.

I am aware that the above examples represent a reasonably rose-tinted view of some of the things that have arisen as a result of the kids having two homes, but I genuinely believe that these exemplify another key facet of establishing shared-parenting.

> ***Shared-parenting is not just a means of making the best out of a bad situation. It is also a positive thing that when properly established (with purpose, planning and when allowed to mature with the passing of time) can give rise to numerous benefits and positive impacts for the kids and parents alike.***

Whilst this is not a Golden Rule as such, I have highlighted this point as it is something that I am really keen for you to absorb and understand; I believe in it whole-heartedly.

The freedom to come and go

Getting back to the various aspects of the logistics of shared-parenting, I want to spend a few minutes on the concept of structured-rigidity that I introduced earlier in the book. As you will be aware by now there are a number of quite structured ways in which our shared-parenting arrangement has been put together with the intention of doing what we felt was the best for the kids. An aspect of the logistical side of things is in relation to how much flexibility can be granted to kids to 'come and go' within the structures of that arrangement.

Time has passed and my eldest daughter has started to show an interest in spending time independently with her friends along with the responsibility to be granted this freedom. As such we decided jointly to occasionally let her spend time with friends in the local town centre to go for a hot chocolate, to window shop or to go and see a movie. Within this we are also keen to encourage her within bounds the freedom to call by at each parent's home in weeks when she is staying with the other. This is obviously something that requires a certain acceptance of the fact that at a certain age, children become young adults and as such cannot be dictated to which of their homes they can go to at a given time if they are to truly consider them homes. This is however still managed within the bounds of maintaining the structure of alternate weeks for where the kids are actually in residence. I think this raises a few key points.

Having a certain degree of freedom to come and go to a degree teaches independence and self-confidence as well as a sense of belonging and association with the homes. The balance for this though is in ensuring that they realise and respect that specific to our circumstances, both Jo and I work at home some of the time, hence it is not always possible or convenient for them to come and go unannounced since this could conceivably be disruptive where we are working and require quiet and concentration.

A further complication to this is that inevitably due to our personal circumstances, social activities are often arranged around the time when the kids will be with the other parent and so it may not always be convenient to just pop-in in case this interferes with things such as friends visiting or such-like that may otherwise not be undertaken were the kids present. I am struggling to phrase this without giving the impression that I get up to particularly nefarious or unsavoury activities at home when the kids aren't with me, which is not the case! As they get older, the children have been given more freedom to pop by for a visit when they are with the other parent, but we've agreed that this shouldn't be done unannounced and instead they should call or text ahead of times to see if someone is in, and if so, whether it is convenient.

Linked to the above, we have over time determined that it works best for us to have keys held to each other's homes. This is primarily as a means of ensuring that in the case that the kids desperately need something from their other home, that they can gain access. This is not the same as providing any-time access to the home to the kids and my ex, but is used with caution and with the proviso that we will call or text ahead in the extreme case that the key needs to be used. Again, the use of such access is only by prior warning or agreement and whether you will want to employ a similar approach with your ex for the kids' purposes is really up to you. The key thing to bear in mind is that like all other aspects of shared-parenting, the main driver is in doing what is best for the kids. Golden Rule #1 drives all things.

Looking to the future

One final thing to touch on in the consideration of all things logistical is in relation to how things may change in the future. With greater responsibility and mobility for kids comes an increased opportunity to abuse the freedom! I have always feared from day one as a parent, the day when either of my daughters might do as virtually all of us will have done at some point and told their parents that they will be in one place whilst intending to be in quite another. Some get away with it, some don't and unfortunately the consequences of such deceptions can range from a vaguely annoyed parent and a chastised child, to consequences arising for the child that don't bear thinking about. What I am mindful of is that in a shared-parenting arrangement there will exist potentially greater scope at some point in the future for the child (or more realistically, the teenager) to say to Mum that they are staying at Dad's, to say to Dad that they are staying at Mum's, and to then be somewhere else completely different. A terrifying notion!

All I can say at this point when the possibility of this occurrence is still (hopefully) some way off, is that it is my deepest hope that both the trust and open communication that I have attempted to build up with my kids since it was possible to talk and reason with them will limit the extent to which this is a threat. Furthermore, the open lines of communication that I have similarly attempted to encourage with their Mum via our shared-parenting of them will ensure that we have at least some chance of rumbling such schemes before they come to fruition. I think, realistically that there will no doubt be new and cunning scams that are brought to bear over the next few years by my daughters as they discover the freedoms that they are on the cusp of as young adults, and as such all I can do is the same as any parent, and be as vigilant as possible and trust in the character of the young person who I have raised.

Chapter 7 – The doubters, the nay-sayers and the detractors

At this point, let us revisit the key motivations for establishing a shared-parenting arrangement.

You have entered into a relationship with another person, and presumably at some point that relationship has been underpinned by love enough that you have sought to pro-create. At some point thereafter you have ceased to be in love with your partner, and so take the bold and brave decision that the relationship must end, but that you want to remain an active parent responsible for your offspring on equal terms as their other parent. All of this is a normal sequence of events, and probably accounts for the vast majority of people in relationships that fail, within which there have been children born. The main difference between the conventional approach and that which I am advocating in this book, is in how this desire to continue to amicably and jointly parent the kids is translated into shared-parenting, or whether the intentions play little part in the arrangement that is ultimately struck.

One of the things I genuinely believe is that you both, as the child's parents are the model for their view of human relationships. They will learn from you what it is to be a father or mother, husband or wife, provider or home-maker. They will learn from your actions the importance of being happy in yourself, and doing what you can to make others around you happy, the importance of being part of a team in a family or relationship. They will observe from how you act whether it is acceptable to shout at others or be shouted at, to seek companionship and be happy, to demonstrate your affection through physical contact, and that it is okay to demonstrate your emotions whether by laughter or through tears. Through the parting of their family they will also learn first-hand that relationships fail and that people come into and out of their lives. I was devastated when I first considered that in parting from their mother I had taught my girls that relationships don't last. I was worried that I had taken away from the kids the opportunity to grow up in a happy, cohesive and stable family environment. I have realised in the years since that there is far more to it than is represented in that simplistic view.

In parting from their Mum and establishing the arrangement we have, I believe that we have demonstrated to kids that although relationships do fail, it is possible to salvage the best bits of it and preserve a happy, albeit non-traditional family environment. I believe we have also demonstrated that it is okay to move on in life if something isn't perfect and you can change it if you are willing to put the effort into making that happen and manage the inevitable emotional pain that will come with the process of finishing the relationship. This is not the same as teaching them that relationships are disposable things that should be cast aside when they are not giving you what you want, but more that as humans we have a right to pursue happiness and a responsibility to ourselves for pursuing this state, and a responsibility to others as to how we treat them during this process.

I have heard a view from parents where they have parted from their ex and have kids that they are trying to raise in a variety of different parenting arrangements, that they feel tremendous guilt and that in splitting up they have already destroyed their kids views on how relationships will be. I think that the converse is true; I genuinely believe all the points I've made above about being the model for your kids views on relationships but I also believe it is in the *how* as well as the *what* you do that shapes their views.

My parents lived the proverbial perfect marriage and are still together to this day. They taught me numerous lessons about being in a relationship and about being a person more generally that have helped shape the person that I am, and yet the model of their relationship (a long, happy and stable marriage) didn't predicate the way that my marriage would work out. Fundamentally I learned from them the importance of treating others as you wish to be treated, the value of happiness, and of seeing something through even if you know it is going to be difficult. These are all values and approaches that I believe I have adopted in my life and demonstrated consistently, including in the formulating of my shared-parenting arrangement with my ex-wife.

My point in saying all of the above is to hopefully refresh our memories as to what we are trying to achieve when we consider and subsequently set in place a shared-parenting arrangement. That whilst the relationship has failed, we are still motivated to do the best we can for the kids and are still keen to provide the best possible environment within which to raise them and teach them the best values we can, as well as the most positive facets of human relationships.

I don't think that any reasonable person could disagree with the above motives or aspirations since they demonstrate a focus on:

- Not being defeated by circumstance; that just because the relationship has failed, all is not lost either in terms of giving the kids the best possible family structure and home life that we can.
- Still wanting to demonstrate Mum and Dad as positive role-models for relationships which I contend can be done on an equal footing with those whose relationships do not fail and which are 'as solid as a rock'.
- Being sufficiently focussed on doing the absolute best for the kids whilst not losing sight of the fact that the relationship *has* failed and that both Mum

and Dad are moving forwards with their lives to make themselves happy as well.

I have therefore found somewhat surprising the objections that I've encountered in relation to shared-parenting. I won't begin to pretend that it's a constant barrage of criticism or disgust by any means since I am pleased to say that for the most part feedback seems to be extremely positive. As stated previously, shared-parenting is the opposite end of the spectrum from being the easy option following the breakdown of a relationship, and so plaudits are often given for taking an approach that maximises one's time with the kids, and places them at the centre of considerations as to how to move life forwards.

Positive feedback also usually centres around admiration for Jo and I for having put aside our differences to focus instead on doing the right things for the kids. However, it is undeniable that there have also been comments and feedback that I have encountered that demonstrate a negative view in some ways. I have summarised these, along with my interpretations and comments below. One of the curses of being a 'thinker' is that I have obviously spent hour-upon-hour mentally dissecting the comments made by others, often at the cost of a sleepless night of worry!

Kids need their Mum first, and their Dad second

I want to explicitly state at this point that it is not my intention to get embroiled in the debate over the rights of fathers in estranged families, both since this is an extremely complex and emotive area and not one that I feel I can add much of value or insight to based on my personal experience. As mentioned above, one of the assumptions for entering into shared-parenting is that both parents are equal and willing participants in the arrangement. However, I raise this topic in passing since I believe it can contribute to some of the views expressed by detractors as a negative of shared-parenting.

This view tends to arise for a number of reasons and from a variety of parents. It can come from Mums who want to justify the (undisputed in my view) importance of their role; a role that I genuinely believe in some individuals can be magnified to such a dangerous degree that it can subsume most other aspects of their being and effectively become their identity as a whole. It is understandable that at a time where they have lost their relationship and their ego is probably hurting that they would wish to cling to other roles in their life as the things that define them to a significant degree and which they are no doubt very proud of and good at. Nonetheless, it can be a view that blinkers somewhat their ability to see the role that both Dad and Mum can, and should play in the raising of both girls and boys.

I have also found that Dads can be prone to expressing this view as well. I think this can be motivated by a genuine agreement with the view above expressed by Mum, but in at least some instances it is also propagated by the Dad in a family playing a more passive or side-lined role, such that his confidence in the role of Dad is that of a supporting 'extra' rather than a lead in its own right. It could also be motivated by a desire to not be involved in shared-parenting either through a lack of desire, or simply a lack of confidence in his ability to fulfil 50% of the parenting role on his own, either practically or conceptually.

The final observation that I have made in relation to detractors who raise this point is that they can often be the parents of kids that are rather more clingy or dependent on their Mum than they might be if they were a bit more confident as kids generally. This is certainly not a criticism of either mother or child in this instance, but it is merely an observation on a trait I have observed often. Whilst kids can be pretty clingy to Dad at times, it is more usual in my experience that Mum will be the one who is called on by kids when things get tough! That said I have known many kids who seem to preserve this clinginess long beyond when it would normally be expected to have been grown out of. Such Mums are bound to express this view based on their personal experience and on a psychological level I would guess that it gives them a sense of feeling wanted and needed, feeding their ego. I always wonder to myself if they are really doing their kids a favour by allowing this clinginess to pervade beyond a certain age, and if in fact it doesn't secretly feed that very need that suits the Mum's own agenda on an on-going basis?

On the point about age, I would like to just touch on one caveat and say that whilst I genuinely disagree with this detracting view (and will state why in a minute), there is a little more substance to it in instances where the kids are younger. As I have previously mentioned, I think there is clearly a point when the kids are very young that if you were contemplating shared-parenting this might be rather more difficult to establish due to the age of the child. I won't discuss the details of this again as it has already been covered, but suffice to say that earlier than the age of 4 there is probably some merit in considering whether the kids are really ready to be parted from Mum for a full week at a time. It really does depend on the maturity and independence of the child though so I offer this only as a suggestion, not a hard and fast rule.

In relation to why I think that this detracting view is somewhat flawed, I would mostly point to my own personal experience. Fundamentally I believe that human beings in general can show tremendous resourcefulness, skill and capability whether it is called upon in the face of adversity or merely when they are motivated to rise to a challenge. I have now been a single-parent to two girls from ages ranging from 4 to 16 (so far) and have ridden the crashing waves of a sea of parental challenges ranging from the day-to-day stuff such as the dietary foibles and progression away from nappies and dummies in a toddler, up to and including runaway cases of head-lice, swine 'flu, playground spats and jealousies, puberty, periods and the need to purchase sanitary products at short notice. My usual caveat of others no doubt having to deal with much worse does of course still apply. My point though is that all these things which might otherwise have been dealt with by Mum in a traditional family setting, have been taken in my stride and managed with little in the way of fanfare or upset. When you have no choice but to get on with and deal with things, you do so. Challenges that are peculiar to boys or to girls will both no-doubt get different treatment at the hands of Mum than by Dad, but the bottom line is that they get treated. They get dealt with. When the going gets tough, the tough do indeed get going.

The other pertinent point in response to this objection is that if you are truly operating a co-operative, communicative shared-parenting arrangement then in fact the involvement of both parents is preserved and there is no reason why one or other parent (or indeed, the kids) cannot call on each other to sense-check something or seek guidance or input. I know that my eldest daughter will call on her Mum to discuss things that she feels she wants to discuss with her instead of me. I don't get affronted by it (in fact, I am somewhat relieved in many ways depending on the topic!) However, I also know that my ex is not judging my abilities as a parent based on the fact that she has to be consulted when the kids are with me, since Golden Rule #1 underpins it all and it is simply another piece of evidence that our arrangement is based on what is best for the kids.

Hopefully this rather impassioned response to the detractor about kids needing their mother first, will emphasize to you that I don't disagree with the viewpoint outright, but rather that I would contend that fathers can be equally capable, and that in some instances it might just be to the child's (and the parents') benefits when both parents get equally involved in their lives to an extent that might not otherwise come about in a conventional family set-up.

Kids need a single place to call home

I have discussed my views on this previously. This statement, when expressed as a detractor is usually based around the person trying to clutch at the obvious points why shared-parenting isn't 'right', a standpoint that feels that what is conventional is the only possible way of doing things. The baseline for convention is clearly for the child to reside in a single home with both parents. What is conventional for families who have parted would then presumably comprise the main home being with one or other parent, and the child then having a room or space at the other parents' home for evening or weekend visits? This is of course the convention that has been established over time for the majority of separated families where a degree of civility still exists, and it preserves the notion of the child having one place to live in and call home and another space that they visit. For many people, convention and the traditional ways of doing things still carry enormous weight and rightly or wrongly shape their views on how things should be done. I find this a remarkably backward view, and whilst I am certainly not someone who believes in challenging convention or doing things differently just for the sake of it, I equally have no issue with trying something new if I believe there may be benefits to be gained from doing so.

I have also discussed earlier in the book the lengths that we have gone to do try and establish both homes with equal status so that the kids feel like they simply have two main homes rather than one that is temporary and the other that is the main home. Indeed, if you ask my kids on a given day they may even tell you that they have a third home, that being with my parents, their grandparents, who live at the other end of the country from us and at which they each have their own rooms decorated for them and filled with their things. As such, I counter this view by stating that it is a matter of how the individual homes are treated and how the kids are conditioned to adapt to the multiple places where they spend their time. I for one would rather raise kids who have a degree of flexibility over where they find themselves when they put their head on the pillow and are able to associate comfort, stability and security as being driven from the love, support *and* the physical environment that they find themselves in, rather than it purely being about being in one single place that they are told is home. Shared-parenting has been a convenient way of instilling this view in my kids, and it has given them a valuable ability to be flexible, adaptable and resourceful.

You want to have your cake and eat it
I characterise this view as being centred around the perception that the shared-parenting arrangement is driven solely by a belief that it is motivated by Mum and Dad's own selfish ends. The detractors will usually express that you are pushing the kids back and forth to suit your own convenience, making yourselves feel better for having equal contact, and trying to also have 50% of your time free as well.

On the one hand I can see where this perception could come from (although I would hope that anyone who genuinely knew me or my ex would not really believe that we could be motivated by such things) in that it would appear superficially to offer numerous benefits for both Mum and Dad as well as for the kids. Quite why this is a bad thing I don't know, and can only assume that the detractors would rather a custody or parenting arrangement had a reasonable amount of deprivation and penitence built into it in order to make sure that everyone was thoroughly miserable?

I think that whilst the view might be expressed quite genuinely and with some conviction, it is also prompted in part at least by a degree of jealousy rather than outright cynicism towards the 50/50 arrangement. This view will usually come from single parents in arrangements where they feel they are making up for the inadequacies of their ex (who presumably is either not willing or able to take on more responsibility or couldn't be trusted to do so adequately to meet the needs of the kids either genuinely, or in their view). I can understand and empathise with the sentiment and how it arises but I wholeheartedly disagree with the assertion that anyone entering into shared-parenting arrangements would be motivated by anything ahead of what was best for the kids.

My responses to this point of view are generally voiced as follows:

- I contend that the structured 50/50 approach is far more considerate to a child's feelings and their inherent need for stability, cohesion and a feeling of comfort with the arrangements that surround their life, than other more convoluted arrangements whereby the kids are with Mum most of the time, but with Dad on a Wednesday night, and on alternate weekends, and sometimes for school holidays. This is of course a fictional example, but not that uncommon I'd suggest where courts have not decreed the access arrangements or Mum and Dad have determined what suits them.
- I have also alluded in Golden Rule #4 to my genuine belief that it is okay for Mum and Dad to arrive at an arrangement that suits them, as long as the other Golden Rules (primarily #1 of course) are met. I firmly believe that as long as the kids are put first in any arrangement it is also fine for Mum and

Dad to arrive at an arrangement that allows them their own lives as well. No-one would surely criticise a married couple who were committed to ensuring that each was given equal free time to rest, recuperate and pursue hobbies and interests around the kids and I see little difference in this instance where the time is available for Mum and Dad to devote to other aspects of their lives. Speaking for myself, the time that I have in the weeks when the kids are not with me is well spent catching up on personal administration, housework and on hobbies and my social life which ensures I am in the best possible state to be a full time father when they are with me. A happy Toby equals a happy Dad!

- Finally, I would once again counter with the position that shared-parenting is far from being the easy or convenient option and requires the greatest magnitude of equal commitment on the part of both parents in order to make it work than any other mix of parenting where the responsibility and effort is always going to be skewed towards one or other parent, and seldom arrives at the best solution for the children.

My intention in outlining the objections that I have encountered above is not a political attempt to sway anyone towards shared-parenting who isn't in favour of it or a bid to ease some sort of guilt on my own-part. I firmly believe that as with most aspects of adapting to change, whatever change that may be, it requires all parties to be firmly bought-into what they are doing, to really understand and believe in what they are doing and to be committed to making it a success. The discussion above is perhaps better used as a means of challenging your own thinking on matters pertinent to shared-parenting, to assist you in figuring out if you really want to enter into such an arrangement and to perhaps assist those around you (your ex, your friends or your extended family) in understanding how and why you think this might be suitable for you and your kids.

Chapter 8 – Hints and tips for ongoing success

This chapter is intended to draw together a number of lessons, hints and tips that I have picked up during the last 10+ years of living in the shared-parenting arrangement. Whilst the individual points do not perhaps warrant an entire chapter in their own right, and in some cases are not sufficiently deserving of a 'Golden Rule' I believe they are nonetheless useful as hints that might make your shared-parenting a little easier.

Dealing with employers

One of the potentially most challenging practical aspects of living a shared-parenting arrangement once you have put it in place is for both parents in managing their careers and in making this aspect of their life work alongside their parenting role. This is another example where the individual circumstances of each person will differ significantly which makes it difficult to generalise on how to make things work. I think though, that there are some basic principles that can be applied to everyone's circumstances.

Once you have agreed upon a shared-parenting arrangement with your ex you will have agreed the means by which this is funded between you. For the purposes of simplicity in this discussion, it is assumed that you have agreed a 50/50 split of the kids' time, and that both parents work equally (whether this is full time, or part time). The basis for stating these details as assumptions is that each parent aspires to be financially independent of each other and to pursue their careers individually in much the same way as they were intending to within the bounds of their relationship. The reason I say this is that I believe that alongside the principles of shared-parenting aligned to being the best parent you can be to the kids, there also needs to be consideration of the person being the best person they can be for themselves including furthering your respective careers. Shared-parenting should not be viewed as a reason to have to compromise your career aspirations, instead it should be a means of preserving the career that you were nurturing and developing before you split from your ex, or preferably to broaden your horizons and improve things *if you want to*.

The purpose of adopting this approach is that it sets the precedent for how you will live within the shared-parenting arrangement. It is not that you are setting out merely to get by at work in order to allow you to be the best parent you can be. Instead, your goal should be that in treating your shared-parenting as a given within your life, you are also allowing yourself to pursue your career aspirations and to achieve what you want to achieve in work or in personal development; taking this mind-set from the outset will then shape how you approach work. If you set out for success, then you stand a better chance of achieving it. If your goal is merely to 'get-by' then I'd contend that this is the best you are ever likely to achieve.

It is important that you understand the above distinction and perhaps a couple of examples taken from my own life may assist in illustrating what I mean. I am fortunate to be able to say that my career to-date has been something of a success in that for the most part as the years have gone on I have moved from job to job, usually progressing in terms of gathering experience, learning new things and generally increasing my income on a regular basis either through earning promotions or taking new jobs with larger salaries. I put a certain amount of this down to luck but I also believe that in order for luck to help you out you have to be prepared to receive it and make the most of the opportunities it presents; fortune favours the brave, as the saying goes. Luck is what happens when preparation meets opportunity!

The start of our shared-parenting arrangement coincided with me moving back to Manchester to start a new job, and the job I started was the highest paid that I had taken to that point. I felt that this was yet another vindication of the decision to move back to Manchester since this came at a point where I was certainly in need of the money to make up for the debt I had incurred whilst travelling regularly from Somerset to Manchester and back to see my kids. However, I digress.

The key point was that I was starting a new job, keen to impress and prove my worth, but I was also mindful of the fact that I had to demonstrate my ability in a competitive and pressurised environment whilst also getting to grips very quickly with being a full-time working single father every other week. This was extremely daunting to me. On personal reflection the things that I now identify as aiding in achieving this have been numerous, but include the following:

1) An extremely supportive and reliable child-minder – You will recall from the account of an average school morning in the Hazlewood family home, that things are structured around getting everything done in a reasonably organised fashion. A pivotal role was also played, particularly in the early days by the kids' child-minder who made it possible to get the kids dropped off early in the morning such that I could get to work in good time, get my hours in and then be home to pick them up at a reasonable hour. It wasn't necessary to seek special consideration in making this arrangement and it was all fitted in around standard hours for full-time child-care but the key point was in being open and honest about mine and the kids' needs, outlining how I proposed to make it work, and seeking their agreement to fulfil the child-minding role. Fundamentally, the child-minder is an employee of yours, taken on to provide a service so it is very important whether you use child-minders, nurseries or pre- and post-school clubs to

treat them as such and ensure you get the service you need. Our childminder has since become an extremely important family-friend and I genuinely think that this has arisen in part as a result of us working collaboratively with her and being open and honest about the terms of the arrangement from the outset. It is also thanks in no small-part to her exceptional kindness and good-nature.

2) Being organised– It shouldn't come as any surprise to you by now that organisation, time-keeping, preparation and forward-planning all make things go a lot more smoothly when you are trying to get to work, do your job and be a single-parent around this.

3) Being prepared to start work early in the morning – This is a simple one but not something that will be applicable to all. I am firm believer in starting early in order to make it possible to finish early or on-time. I'd far rather forego an hour of sleep (or more likely an hour of procrastination and time wasting before work) in the morning to ensure that the 8 hours of work that I have to put in are completed whilst there is still a useful period of the day left. This is of course down to your job and whether it is suitable to such flexible hours. The other benefits of this include the potential to beat peak-travel times/rush hours both in the morning and evening which can also be a thief of useful time.

4) Making use of your lunch-breaks and commutes – I have also found that a bit of forward planning can identify personal admin that can be done during a lunch break or perhaps groceries can be bought for the evening meal with the kids, making productive use of the time at your disposal. Alternatively, but equally valid is to use the time as a means of fitting in exercise, meeting up with friends, catching up on reading or any other pursuit that you may feel is in danger of being pushed to the back burner in the mornings and

evenings when the kids will rightly occupy your time. All these suggestions are offered in place of spending an hour walking aimlessly around town centres or browsing the web, which can often become the de-facto way of passing a lunch-hour in the absence of anything else to do. I also mention commutes here on the basis that I used to routinely plan my route home so that I could pick up groceries for that evening on my way to pick the kids up from the child-minder.

5) Reasonable flexibility from your ex – Within the bounds of Golden Rules #2 and #3, it is also useful to have a reasonable degree of flexibility from your ex in allowing you a degree of flexibility to attend meetings at locations that would require travel, or at times when you would normally be looking after your children. Caution needs to be exercised in calling upon this flexibility in order to maintain the boundaries of your shared-parenting arrangement but it is something that can be beneficial for you both if managed effectively, if only as a last-resort safety net.

6) Planning your workload and work calendar – This is simply a case of exerting whatever influence you can to ensure that meetings/training courses/work mandated travel fall within weeks when the kids are with your ex. This is not always possible to influence, but as a general rule the alternate-weeks pattern should make it easy to plan ahead with reasonable accuracy and foresight. A 50-50 shared arrangement on alternate weeks can be plugged into electronic calendars for years ahead, making it really easy to ensure that work commitments aren't inadvertently scheduled for when childcare commitments clash.

The final and most significant factor warrants slightly deeper discussion. I have had a number of jobs and worked for a number of different line managers since I started in our shared-parenting arrangement so I feel confident in suggesting this as a course of action that can aid in allowing you to do your job effectively within your shared-parenting arrangement. The key success factor for me is in being open and honest with your line manager from the outset.

This sounds like a simple and potentially obvious step. However, it is something that I was initially hesitant about doing for a number of reasons. First of all, I am not someone who is naturally comfortable talking with others, especially those I don't know very well about the personal circumstances of my life in a work context. I believe there is value in being able to keep your work life separate from your personal one at least until you have established yourself in a role and people know you better. Furthermore, I was always reluctant to portray myself as someone whose circumstances required that I was treated differently or given any special dispensation to allow me to do my job. I want to be able to do my job to the best of my ability on level terms with my contemporaries and I don't expect or want to be given any special treatments. Finally, I guess that given that the first time I had to discuss these circumstances I was still unsure about how it would all play out since it was new to me. The last thing I wanted to do was to position myself for additional scrutiny, not just as the new guy in a job but also as 'the guy who is just starting out as a single parent'.

Nonetheless, I took what I felt was a bold step and in business-like and concise, non-emotional terms positioned my circumstances along with my proposal for how I intended to make my new job work. In real terms I was actually asking for nothing from my employer that wasn't already within the terms and conditions of my employment. However, the reason why I wanted to be upfront about things was to set expectations and be open about how I intended to do my job to the best of my ability working around my family commitments. My proposal was as follows:

- In the weeks that the kids were with me, I would be working the contractual 40 hours per week, starting routinely at 8.30am and finishing at 5pm (taking half an hour for lunch)
- In the instance of needing to be able to work extended hours to make up time or just to demonstrate willingness, I would utilise the home-working facility provided by my employer to allow access to IT systems remotely via the web
- In the event of the kids being off school sick I would either work from home or take flexible-leave that could be made up during the weeks when they weren't with me.
- In the weeks that the kids were not with me I would have greater flexibility to make up time, work additional hours or attend off-site meetings where these could be scheduled for these weeks.

As you can see, there is nothing radical or revolutionary about this approach or anything overly complex about the proposals that I was making; I also wasn't asking for anything that would be detrimental for my employer to provide.

I believe this worked for the reasons that:

a) I presented my manager with a statement of facts and undertakings that I would take to make my position workable and to ensure that I was able to demonstrate myself as worthy of the job rather than a list of potential problems.
b) I was open and honest from the outset, stating my position from day one of working for that manager rather than waiting for the first time something went wrong (for example one of the kids being off school sick) before bemoaning the constraints of my situation and asking for clemency.

I have taken the above position and approach each time I have started a new job or a new career assignment that has meant a new person to bring up to speed with my circumstance, and I don't think it is coincidence that in each instance my approach has been well received and I have succeeded in the job. To emphasize how this has worked I would like to point out that I have worked in organisations as diverse as within local government where I worked in a fixed location, to financial services where I have routinely travelled nationally and internationally and in each instance the same principles and approaches have allowed me to work effectively and successfully. Crucially, this has been *without* requiring any special treatment or favours, just an open-ness and honesty with the employer. I strongly suggest you try it.

Christmas, Birthdays and Special Occasions

One area that is doubtless a potential source of tension for families as they part and enter into shared-parenting is how things such as Christmas (I mention this since it is the religious festival that we celebrate although the same principles would apply to any other), birthdays and other special occasions/family gatherings are handled. As you hopefully expect from me by now, my main advice would be that the first priority is upon applying Golden Rule #1 and that all else will follow. However, this is something that would hopefully be the case anyway so I will illustrate some of the other experiences that we've had in our family in the last 10 years.

Christmas plays a big part in our family. Like many people this is not due solely to religious beliefs but due to the fact that it is a fun time of year during which we gather together with extended family and enjoy indulgent food and drink with each other and exchange some gifts. I guess it was always going to be a time of year where the pressures to preserve the best of the way things were before we parted was heightened, but also tainted with the fact that things weren't likely to remain the same as they had been due to family circumstances changing significantly.

The first couple of Christmases following my parting from my ex-wife were relatively easy to cater to since her family live close by to our homes in Manchester and mine were scattered around the country and each had their own commitments to fulfil either with elderly relatives or their own extended family. We therefore attempted to maintain a strand of normality for the kids in as much as Jo and her family were kind enough to include me in their family Christmas so that I could be with the kids on Christmas day. At this point we were also still buying the kids' presents jointly so it was also good to be with them on Christmas morning; undoubtedly the high point of the day for kids of all ages!

The obvious benefit of this scenario was that the kids were able to enjoy their Christmas day with both their parents present and I suppose that in some way this eased the transition somewhat. As time has moved on, we have evolved our thinking in this area though such that after a point (the first two Christmases after we parted) when the kids were a little older we felt that this was a reasonable time to start alternating who the kids spent their Christmas with. How we split up the festive period really depends on when Christmas falls and this is the one time of year besides the summer when holidays are taken (more on this later) that the formally structured alternate week system is relaxed a little more to accommodate the holiday. The kids have become accustomed to this pattern and the great thing is that they get to enjoy a semblance of Christmas with both parents individually and with both sides of their extended family. Through the wonders of modern day communications they are still able to speak to or even see the other parent on Christmas day itself, but to be honest we have always encouraged both our kids to try and be 'in the now' and not yearn for either of us when they are with the other.

The underlying fact is that we are always thinking of them when not with them, and we can all reach out to each other if we need or want to but this shouldn't distract them from enjoying the moment of where they are and what they are doing.

The further benefit of the above arrangement for each of Jo and I (Golden Rule #4!) is that we are each able to plan on alternate years to spend Christmas Day exactly how we want and with who we want since we know that our Christmas Day with the kids will come next year on the 25th December and has probably already been 'mocked up' to some extent once already before they headed off with their other parent.

I have encountered numerous arrangements that separated families adopt for Christmas day ranging from still spending the day together, to always having Christmas morning in the same house but then alternating each year for the remainder of Christmas day, through to a similar alternate-years approach as me. The key thing will be that Christmas and other similar events and times of year will hold different significance to different families depending on how they celebrate such events and other factors such as religious beliefs. The bottom line for me is that provided Golden Rule #1 is applied then the family will find an arrangement that suits them. The word of caution around this would be to ensure that the arrangement you adopt does not blur the boundaries of your shared-parenting arrangement and is not clouded by implementing something that is actually more driven by what you yourself want out of it (for example, to *always* be able to see your kids on Christmas morning out of your own guilt or sentimentality).

Birthdays fall into the same category and for us have always been treated in much the same way as Christmas; first in that the arrangements we put in place have always been driven by what was best for the kids, and then subsequently by what we felt would transition the separation of our family in the kindest way for the kids. Birthdays hold less significance in our family but we do of course still celebrate them with gusto and attempt to make the birthday boy or girl feel special for a day. As such, I have always attempted to make sure that I see the kids on their birthday in years when it falls on a day that they are with their Mum, and vice versa. The only key difference that has evolved in the arrangements over time has been in relation to the celebrations that accompany these events.

When the kids were younger the traditional birthday celebration would usually be organised (comprising of gathering together the birthday girl and 10 or so of her close-friends to scream, run-around and generally get over-excited in a 'play centre' or some such other venue featuring soft-play facilities and a stroke-inducing white noise of kids generally 'expressing themselves'). In the spirit of fairness and parity we funded these equally and jointly and both attended to try and make it run as smoothly as possible. The choice of celebrations has changed slightly as they've got older and I'm relieved to say, become a little more sophisticated (towards a meal and movie with friends). The approach for me and Jo has remained the same; we fund it equally and both attend if the birthday girl deems that we are required.

Finally, in relation to other celebrations and events it is fair to say that flexibility is key. I am thinking here of other family occasions (such as a family wedding or birthday on either mine or Jo's side). Assuming there is no good reason not to accommodate a request for the kids to spend time with their Mum at some event should they be with me when one of these events falls, I have no reason to object and as such the requests are always indulged, and vice-versa.

I'm conscious that I have harped-on about Golden Rule #1 extensively, but it really is a useful guide in all aspects of shared-parenting and offers a useful acid-test against which to establish if a particular response to a question or issue is appropriate. If my ex were to ask she could 'borrow' the kids to attend a relative's surprise birthday party, the bottom line would be that the kids would enjoy it and I would be unlikely to have anything planned that couldn't be rearranged to accommodate this, hence the right answer (satisfying Golden Rule #1) would be a resounding 'yes'. Similarly, if my daughter's birthday fell in her week with me and I decided that I would take the girls out for dinner to celebrate, should she ask if she could invite her Mum and her Mum's partner along too it would be putting my own needs and preferences ahead of my daughters if I were to say 'no'. Golden Rule #1 will always ensure that the right thing is done for your child and hence for your shared-parenting arrangement!

Family holidays

In common with many other facets of our shared-parenting arrangement, the planning and taking of family holidays is something that has evolved over time. In our first year apart the first summer came round just a few months of me living in Somerset. We decided that a positive family holiday for the girls would be for Jo to bring the kids down to my house and for us to spend a few days taking day trips in the local area by way of a pseudo family holiday. On reflection this was backed by a positive intent and in a number of ways served benefit in terms of giving the kids something different to do in an environment they would normally only have shared with me. However, I think it also gave rise to some other interesting learning points.

First of all, and I have noticed this as an enduring factor that remains to this day, the kids do behave slightly differently when they are around both Jo and I than they do when they are alone with me. I don't mean this as a criticism for I think it is entirely natural that children's behaviour is driven both by their upbringing but also by adapting to the environment and surroundings in which they find themselves. I remember thinking back then in the summer of 2006 that it must be somewhat confusing for them after adapting to at least 5 months of Jo and I seldom being around them and each other in the same place, to all of a sudden be in a home environment with us both present (albeit sleeping in separate rooms I hasten to add). Nonetheless, we did what we set out to do and spent some time doing fun things together. I guess that this was largely a success in that the girls had some fun, but it was also the last time that we spent a prolonged period of time together, the 4 of us and I think that since then the approach to holidays has been what would be considered more realistic and pragmatic.

We are now in a pretty settled pattern whereby the kids have a 2-week holiday with Jo and her family in the summer (which obviously requires some relaxing of the week-on, week-off structure) but which usually falls at the same time each year. Separately to that, I take a holiday with the girls at some point each year where we go away, usually with my extended family, and then there will be numerous other trips and weekends away which punctuate the year. This is probably nothing unreasonable or unusual to expect but it demonstrates to me that a holiday with Mum and Dad is no more expected or yearned for by my kids than it would be if we weren't in a shared-parenting arrangement. They know how things work and they are extremely happy with that since the trips are planned as family holidays in both instances with one or other half of their family. All kids really seem to need from a holiday in most cases is access to a pool or beach, a ready supply of ice cream and a bit of pocket money, and the opportunity to stay up a bit later than usual and it seems to me that most of their wants and needs are filled!

Fundamentally, there is no reason why a shared-parenting arrangement needs to change this. Perhaps the only concession that is needed is for a little flexibility on the part of the two parents to accommodate the booking of holidays if this potentially upsets the established schedule of weeks between the two homes.

There are a number of other things that I could note down in relation to things I have learned or points to consider, but many of these will be little more than trivia to most readers since they are quite specific to my situation. The points above summarise some of the key things that I've learned through the life of our shared-parenting arrangement to-date and the key principles that pervade; further evidence (if any were needed) that consideration of most things alongside Golden Rule #1 will generally serve you well. The next chapter looks at one specific other area of my life that I believe has had a significant impact on my shared-parenting arrangement (and vice-versa); dating!

Chapter 9 – Dating and the single parent

Within this chapter I intend to share some of the experiences I have had in relation to dating and the pursuit of a new relationship following my parting from Jo; this spans both the time before starting of our shared-parenting arrangement when I had moved away following our split, and more recently since moving back to Manchester. It is not intended to be a full breakdown and analysis of the trials and tribulations of my dating and love life since;

a) That is not the purpose of this book, and its significance and relevance is mainly in relation to its influence in my life in the context of parenting;
b) I have enough stories in relation to this area to fill another book entirely which, although potentially inflammatory in its content will no doubt be written at some point if only for the catharsis of getting it out of my system; watch this space!

Assuming that you are reading this book in the hope that it may be of some interest or significance to you in your life, it is possible that you could be at any stage in the process of parting from your partner and someway along in the process of considering or establishing a shared-parenting arrangement. Alternatively you may be reading this merely out of interest and because you want to know what I have to say. In either case I would hope that as someone who clearly has an interest in human interpersonal relationships you will not consider me too outlandish or off-the-wall when I express the belief that most if not all of us need someone else in our lives; a partner, a best friend with which to spend our time, to share the highs and lows and to play that role of essentially enriching our lives.

I'm more than happy to accept that this is true to varying degrees for each and every person, since some people are remarkably independent, self-reliant and more than able (happy even) to proceed through life on their own whereas others genuinely seem to need someone else to complete them. I think that I personally fall into the former category but will say that coming out of my relationship with Jo and subsequently as life moved on I went through a number of varying feelings on the matter.

Upon agreeing that we'd split and before the reality sank in, I suppose that I was feeling a mix of relief for having made the difficult decision to part, and alongside the sadness that would emerge as the gravity of the forthcoming change sank in possessed a certain excitement and exhilaration over the possibilities that this presented for a new start. I don't mean this as a slight towards Jo since it wasn't a sense of thinking that I could find a new partner who was 'better' than her as such. I just felt that it was an opportunity to put into place some of the things that I had learned about myself and the things that I needed in a relationship to enrich my life. This sense of excitement and exhilaration also carried into other elements of life. Whilst it was an extremely daunting prospect to imagine starting over in life, essentially moving to a new town, a new job and a new structure around my relationship with the kids which would see me parted from them for lengthy periods of time, there was also an element of genuinely appreciating the clean-slate that life had presented to me with a chance to change things for the better and to make the most of the opportunity.

Getting used to the idea

My initial reaction once we had formally decided to end our marriage was in feeling acceptance of the forthcoming change, perhaps even a slight exhilaration over it, but then feelings of denial over what was really happening and subsequently resistance to that change kicked in. These were manifested not in actions to reverse the change or to prevent it from going ahead since I knew that this was the thing that needed to happen for mine and Jo's benefits and for the kids. This didn't stop me from internally resisting the idea that my marriage was over and that things needed to move on for all of our benefits. On my positive days I would proceed with planning and undertaking the actions that would allow me to move on in life, but on the days when denial and resistance were prominent in my mind it became difficult to accept the way that things were, and to allow myself to proceed with putting the plan in action.

This was particularly difficult in relation to contemplating, let alone enacting changes regarding relationships; it is hard to contemplate a new one when you are not fully over the old one or still taking the steps necessary to exit it! This feeling has since been borne-out by the ending of other relationships I have been in and evidenced also through conversations with friends and family who have been in relationships that have failed (a group which includes virtually everyone I know aside from those anomalies who seem to end up spending their lives with their first-loves!) In simple terms I characterise this sense as feeling reluctance to let go of your old relationship. Once you have been away from the person for a while, you start to fixate on the positives of that relationship, forget the negatives and start to worry that what you had is as good as it's ever going to get. At times like these you just have to trust in your instinct that brought you to this point and trust in your resilience that will get you past it.

I won't take you through a day-by-day, month-by-month analysis of my changing feelings in regard to potentially entering the world of dating and the gradual opening my mind to the possibility of eventually meeting someone new who I could spend my life with. Suffice to say that it was a lengthy and time consuming process that included many about-turns ranging from "I don't need anyone, I can make it on my own" through to "I am nothing without a partner to share my life with" and everything in between. A significant period of time had passed (as I recall at least 6 months after I had moved away from Manchester and both Jo and I were well established in our new lives) before I first contemplated the pursuit of dating and relationships as a possibility in my life.

It had taken for time to pass to essentially get through the grieving process associated with the loss of my relationship and to come out of the other side realising that life was indeed carrying on and things were actually not too bad in the world. In this time I had started to accept the situation more fully and allowed myself the mental space and freedom explore the possibilities that lay before me. I had started to actually feel some hope that things would change for the better. Finally, I would commit fully to the change having happened and this being my new life.

And so it was, the summer of 2006 when I finally felt that I was ready to unleash myself on the world of dating once again. Exciting stuff.

Back in the market

I mentioned earlier in the book that it took Jo and I a few years after we had parted before we actually got divorced. This was not related to any long-term hope or aspiration on either of our parts to get back together at some point. In reality it was simply the case that the least significant aspect of us having been together for me at least, was whether we were legally married or not. When we took the decision to part it was certainly administrative red-tape that needed to be addressed at some point but it was not a high priority for either of us. Crucially, we had struck our own arrangements for the dissolution of our mutual finances and most importantly for the on-going parenting of our kids. Based on that we didn't really need to involve courts, lawyers or other intermediaries in getting set up the structures that would allow us to move forwards with our lives.

Eventually of course it was something that we got done but I undertook to do the majority of the legal paperwork and filing myself with the limited assistance of an online legal service. When the final decrees were granted and the fees paid, Jo and I took the kids out for a curry and toasted our mutual future success and gave ourselves a little self-congratulatory pat on the back for resolving it amicably and with minimal hassle.

Anyway, the point of that digression was to explain my situation when embarking back in the world of dating; I did so as a man separated from his wife and with two kids and a convoluted parenting arrangement. This meant that most weekends were taken up with travelling to and from Manchester to see my kids, and that most of my money was also devoted to trying to make the life I was living a possibility. Quite the catch, I think you'll agree…

As many who know me will testify, I am not skilled in the arts of banter, seduction or of 'chatting-up' women. That I met Jo through my sister is a good illustration of the avenues through which I'm accustomed to meeting women (as problematic and inappropriate as those may be). Don't get me wrong, once I'm in contact with a woman, in conversation, and a rapport has been established I would like to think that my personality and somewhat limited and undoubtedly 'functional' charms kick-in, but it is in the opening that I lack ability, rather than in the closing!

With a heightened self-awareness and a genuine desire to play to my strengths whilst acknowledging my weaknesses I opted for an approach that would offer the best fit; I launched myself on the world of online dating.

A virtual-me

The notes and pointers that I have included in relation to my experiences of dating are intended in the same spirit as the rest of the book, to collate some of the lessons I have learned in case they can be of some use to others.

The first of these summaries is in relation to why I chose to go down the route of online dating. These range from relatively simple factors such as the amount of time and money that I had available to me to lavish on dating. Put simply I really didn't have the time to 'kiss a few frogs' (or whatever the male equivalent is) since my free time and hence that which I could devote to prospectively finding a girlfriend was extremely limited. There was great appeal in being able to sift through profiles until I found some that seemed on screen at least, to be good matches. Similarly, and perhaps most importantly there was little that needed to be done initially other than getting a profile written, and a few decent pictures of me up on the site (by decent, I don't mean clothed... I mean 'doesn't make me look like Shrek'... although I should add that I was also fully clothed in all pictures I have ever used). ALWAYS use pictures of you fully clothed. Top tip.

Online dating also seemed to me the most appropriate option since first and foremost it gave me the chance to outline from-the-off what I felt were the complexities and intricacies of my personal situation. I could also give an overview of the pre-requisites that I felt I needed to be upfront about as needing from a prospective date. I hope I am not unique in feeling that it is essential to be upfront about what you are all about in dating terms (assuming you are genuinely looking for a possible partner, and not any one of a number of other arrangements, liaisons or encounters that many seem to use online dating to facilitate!)

Life has taught me that if you are not certain about who you are, what makes you tick and what you are all about then it is impossible to really feel certain that you are ever going to have met the right person when you do meet someone. How can they be complementary to you if you are not sure who 'you' really is? I have also learned that in any way compromising on the very basic things that you know and believe about yourself and what you want will only lead to problems.

I am not suggesting that any reasonable person should be inflexible or unwilling to change and accommodate their significant other. One of the true measures of having met 'the one' must surely be that you feel complete acceptance of the other person and a willingness to do anything that you can to make them happy, including elements of compromise. I feel that all people will have an absolute baseline of 'essentials' that they want and need out of life and a potential partner and if these essentials are not met or require compromise on either person's part, then an enduring relationship will be difficult to maintain.

Anyway, back to the story… Through some carefully crafted words I felt that I was able to get together a profile that adequately painted the picture of who I was, how my life was shaped and what I was looking for. The feedback I have gathered over time on this (from dates I have been on, and knock-backs I have received to emails that I have sent to prospective dates who courteously declined) has been that my openness and honesty was appreciated and that my profile did at least show that I had bothered to put some thought into it, to try and portray who I am with some accuracy and insight. I encourage a similar openness and honesty to anyone else in my situation. Assuming that you are looking towards meeting a possible partner and/or entering into a relationship rather than looking for a casual liaison then I see absolutely nothing to be gained from not being completely open and honest from the off. I am not suggesting that a profile should reveal everything about you or that you should feel a pressure to provide superfluous detail. Speaking hypothetically about my own situation, there would seem little point in me having suggested that the kids dominated less of my time and resources than they did, since the truth would have come out almost immediately if I got as far as arranging a first date! Similarly, I would rather meet someone to whom the steps I had taken to retain a role in my kids' lives was considered a positive factor rather than a constraint that they could put up with. It is certainly borne-out by my experience that openness is key.

Making the approach

With a number of years' experience of online dating and a number of friends in a similar position you won't be surprised that I have spent a bit of time discussing it, and comparing success (and more often, failure) stories with them. There are a number of ways in which our approaches have differed over time; some favour particular sites, some believe in going on lots of first-dates with matches that they have a scant amount of knowledge about whereas others are more inclined to get to know possible matches through email and even telephone conversations before meeting up.

What we are all united on though is the merits of not merely taking a passive approach to online dating, not of waiting for people to approach you but instead of making the first move. Depending on the site you favour that may be through the simple 'swiping left' as they appear on the screen of your phone via an app, sending of an email, ticking an on-screen box to express interest or actually sending an email to say hello. We are in agreement (and this applies equally to males and females) that it is essential to make the approach and to expect that in many instances you will get ignored or receive knock-backs. The key point is to not be passive and expect people to come to you. This piece of advice whilst not being related to shared-parenting and straying into being more akin to Golden Rule #1 of online dating is mentioned since it was a lesson that was hard-learned in my early days as an online-dater.

I don't believe that I had a specific 'type' in mind when I embarked on online dating. I did however speculate on what I felt were the essential things for a potential match to possess. The list was along the lines of the following:

1) She must be accepting of my having kids and my wanting to be an active part in their lives
2) She must understand that I don't have as much free time to devote to a new relationship as I would otherwise have (indeed, at the outset ¾ of my weekends were devoted to the kids)
3) She must accept that by necessity I still have a lot of involvement with my ex-wife since we are no longer in a relationship together as husband and wife, but we have a joint relationship as parents to the kids
4) Whilst I am not looking for a step-parent for my kids, they must be the kind of person who can get on with kids, enjoy their company and accept their primary role and importance in my life
5) She must also be hot, have an outstanding sense of humour, and find me supremely attractive (somewhat unrelated to my shared-parenting requirements but you'd think me a fraud if I didn't mention it!)

The wish list could have gone on and on, and it probably included much more; the basics though were that acceptance of the role of the kids as outlined in my profile was paramount in order to give any prospective date a chance of developing into a relationship.

In considering the type of woman who would fit this bill this was inevitably down to the individual as to how understanding and accepting she would be of my circumstances. As my time in online dating unfolded my views changed a little in terms of lessons I learned about different 'types' of people that exist.

These types are not intended to be disparaging or clichéd but I mention them since I have found it helpful to be able to draw out some general themes which are driven purely by my attempts to analyse what has made particular matches suitable for me in meeting or not meeting my list of essential characteristics. I have attempted to summarise these types below. They are not based solely on individuals I have encountered but have also been summarised based on traits that have been common to different people. The very nature of human beings is that you cannot fairly summarise them into being a particular type and there are numerous other facets and characteristics that make us who we are. The main thing that I have focussed on though are those traits pertaining to the relationship-needs of the single parent who is looking for a new partner. I believe that they are likely to be relevant to males and females alike.

Single person, no kids
With romanticized rose-tinted glasses on, the optimum route to a relationship would be for two individuals to meet, to fall in love and spend the rest of their lives together as single individuals with no commitments or ties. The individuals would have had no previous relationship history or baggage (or at least nothing so serious as to have resulted in marriages to be entered into or kids to be conceived and born) and the two individuals would remain committed to each other for life. And of course they'd be in love with each other too.

Unfortunately, this is not the way that things tend to go in life and in reality everyone will have their own history, their own emotional baggage and their own memories and belief system based on their life experience to date. As a separated male with two kids from his first marriage, my initial instinct was that the simplest way of meeting my list of essentials would be to meet someone who didn't have their own kids such that there would only be one set of 'complications' brought to the situation; one set of kids to accommodate, one person bringing time constraints to the relationship, and one person whose personal circumstances and history that would complicate things.

I believe that this was sound on the face of it and on paper, it seems to make sense. My experience however, was as follows:

- There is an additional factor at play in that the person who doesn't have kids has no appreciation of the demands of being a parent and as such their ability to understand and empathise with the demands of being a parent can be limited.
- The individual may or may not want to have kids of their own at some point and as such this could be a future source of tension in either respect; Do you want to have more kids at some point? Do you think that someone who doesn't want kids will make a suitable step-parent to yours?

My experience of this type of person has been a mixture of many positives and more than a few negatives. It can be very easy to get swept along with the 'reflected-freedom' of being with someone who doesn't have the constraints on their time that inevitably come with having kids in your life. It makes it far easier to be able to plan to do things for just yourself and the person you are dating since as a rule you only have to find time when you don't have your kids. Similarly it can feel somewhat liberating from the demands of being a single parent to have that feeling that you are effectively going back in time and in some respect dating again without all the grown-up constraints that come when both of you have kids; as such there's at least a 50% reduction in the possibility of conversations revolving around sleepless nights, baby-sitting, the amount of homework that kids get these days, at what age it's acceptable to allow your child access to Facebook and all the other multitude of conversational topics that can proliferate once you're a parent. I for one relish those alternative conversations since being a parent isn't the sole focus of my life, believe it or not.

There are numerous other positive aspects to dating someone who doesn't have kids but these largely hinge on the individual and also on what you want out of a prospective partner. I have known (and dated) women who are keen to be involved in and to support my wider life and commitments related to the kids, and equally others who have no real or immediate desire to play a part in this side of my life and were happy to only see me when my kids-free time allowed. As I outlined in the list of pre-requisites for a potential match above, it has always been important to me that anyone I dated would of course at some point willingly meet the kids and wholeheartedly attempt to form some bond with them. However, depending on the preference of the individual (and I believe that this can evolve as time goes on) I can understand why for someone who you are dating, it could be appealing for them to be enthusiastic to meet your kids as early as possible or equally for them to not be in any great hurry to do so; in either case, the focus would presumably be on both of you bonding with each other and feeling some sense of the relationship being an enduring one long before the kids were drawn into the equation?

Having highlighted some very positive side-effects of dating people who don't have kids, I'd like to highlight some of the negatives or points to note. Again I must emphasize that all of these observations are heavily caveated to emphasize that it will largely be dependent on the individual. Nonetheless, I think that some reasonable generalisations can be made.

As you would probably expect, these individuals will have varying degrees of experience and ability for being around kids. Nobody can really understand all aspects of being a parent until they have first-hand experience of it. I believe that this is equally true for individuals who have grown up with siblings who were much younger than themselves or where their siblings have had kids just as much as those with little or no experience of young kids.

I've also found that those who have grown up in families where the parents were teachers or child minders are no more likely to be guaranteed to possess an innate ability with kids even though they are used to being around other young children.

It *is* challenging as someone who doesn't have kids to adapt to being around young children, especially when those are the children of your prospective partner. I recall in my late teens being around my best friend's baby sister who would cry the minute she saw me, and I recall the mark that left on me (interestingly I continue to have a similar effect on some young kids to this day so perhaps there is something inherently threatening or scary in my appearance or demeanour!) Whilst I appreciate that this example is different to the challenges of being in a relationship with someone who has kids if you don't have them, it is still indicative of the potential pressures that can exist when you try to get-on with kids who are not your own and are not familiar with the challenges that this can present. This is not a criticism since I think it is admirable that any individual should be even conceptually willing to attempt to form a bond with someone else's child under any (well intentioned!) circumstances. I have written the above merely on the basis of having observed it at first-hand.

It can also be difficult for someone without kids to appreciate the degree to which they can dominate and place demands on your time. I learned this in relation to periods where I had the kids for most weekends (before I was in a true shared-parenting arrangement). It was really difficult to allocate time to any potential relationship due to most of my weekends being dominated by the kids, but it has been equally evident since I started shared-parenting too. In addition to the weeks when the kids are with me, there will always be a number of ad-hoc events that crop-up outside of my allocated time to have them (school parents evening and class assemblies, sporting commitments and matches, birthday celebrations, school and family holidays and so-on). Each of these demands my time and attention whether they fall in my week or not. I can fully appreciate that this potential disruption to my plans and time must be frustrating to a potential partner but in my experience those who have kids (whether in established shared-parenting or not) will be far more receptive to and accepting of such disruptions than those who do not have kids.

Something else that is worth discussion at this point is the difficulty that some can have with accepting the reasonably close on-going relationship I have with my ex-wife. Experience has shown that it is really down to the individual as to how trusting they are of me, and secure they are in themselves as to how well they deal with the fact that I have regular communication and contact with my ex-wife. As I hope you appreciate by now, having an effective mechanism for communication and a functional and healthy manner for dealing with your ex-partner is an essential for effectively sharing the parenting of your kids. That is not to say that there should be any blurring of this boundary as regards what remains of your relationship, and the communication needs to be focussed on the fact that you are mutually parenting your kids. It is however a pre-requisite for making the situation work and for the kids to receive the best possible parenting that they can. What cannot be allowed to happen through the introduction of a new partner for one or other of you into the mix is for this to impact or impinge upon the communication you have with your ex. I have learned through bitter and painful experience (more on this later) the effect that this can have and the detrimental impacts it can have for you and your kids. I am keen to suggest that you should guard against this fiercely. Going back to the original point, individuals who I have dated who do not have kids *generally* have much less understanding or tolerance for the essential contact that I have with my ex and will be more likely to have a problem with it.

The final complication that I have experienced in relation to dating those who do not have kids is that they will be more likely at some point to want to have kids of their own. This can be something of absolutely zero consequence to you or alternatively the biggest issue in the world. As such I mention it now with a cautionary tone only. I will discuss later why this can be a major source of tension. Notwithstanding the numerous and serious considerations that this brings with it, this is a possible source of difficulty *if you are not interested in or willing to have more kids at some point.* Presumably this is something that you will have your own clear views on and as such will be able to determine the degree to which this is likely to be a factor for you.

I am reluctant to generalise on the human nature and I realise that we are all individuals with many diverse skills, traits and behaviours. The above observations are merely offered to give insight into some of the things that I have observed and learned over time about a particular type of person.

Single person, with kids in a shared-parenting arrangement (to some degree)
The other basic type that I want to discuss is those who are single (by which I mean separated, divorced, widowed or through any other means or circumstance) and who have kids. I believe there are some traits that are distinct to those where the person shares custody with their ex and others that are specific when the kids have no (or virtually no) contact with their other parent. I have treated these two separately for the purposes of this book.

When I refer to kids in shared-parenting (to some degree), I am bundling together a variety of situations. These may range from arrangements like mine where there is a 50/50 split of the kids' time between both parents. There may be an established sharing of the custody and responsibility (whether 50/50 or biased towards one or other parent). It may be that the kids live the majority of time with one parent but have regular contact with the other (e.g. alternate weekends and perhaps one night in the week). The reason why I bundle all these up together is that based on my experience, when the kids have some degree of regular, voluntary and reasonably amicable access to both parents it signifies something on behalf of the ethos of the parents; like me and my ex they have recognised that in spite of their differences with the other parent of their kids that it is important that contact and regular visitation is maintained for the child's benefit. This ethos then tends to follow through into the understanding and the views that the person will have in regard to the role of kids in your life.

In contrast with my experiences regarding dating people without kids, generally the opposite is true for most traits and characteristics. The overall feeling is usually that the person will have a greater appreciation and empathy to your overall circumstances. They will be more likely to understand the demands that are placed on your time and will appreciate the need for you to have a reasonable amount of contact with your ex in order to manage the life of the kids who you are jointly raising. Paradoxically this is not *always* the case though, and in some cases it can be a source of tension where you have a more civil relationship with your ex than they do. In this instance, feelings of jealousy (presumably) can kick in and problems and differences can arise. Generally though, things are more often accepted and understood regarding the need to communicate with your ex.

In addition to having a greater understanding of the demands that your kids place upon your time and the importance they have in your life, my experience has also shown that for the most part, single parents will themselves be more understanding of and sensitive regarding meeting each other's kids. They will understand the need to carefully balance a desire to meet each other's kids and to become more involved in each other's lives with the fact that first and foremost you are dating each other to build a relationship for your own purposes not in order to build the foundations of a new family unit.

One downside of dating another single parent is the danger of the relationship being formed on the basis of your common experiences as a parent. Based only on my non-scientific observations, there seems to be a tendency when dating another single parent that one can get drawn into discussions and joint musing on the more mundane aspects of single-parenting and this can in turn serve to undermine some of the very reasons why we pursue new relationships in the first place. I am not talking merely about the greater likelihood that your conversations will be centred on aspects of life as a parent or on the fact that inevitably one of the main things that you will initially have in common besides being a single-parent and looking for a new relationship. I guess the degree to which this is a source of difficulty will depend on your own motive for dating and what you are really looking for. Surely though romance and excitement are some of the key motivators in the first place, not just greater opportunities for conversations centred on the joys and challenges of parenting!

Revisiting my own aims and goals, I was certainly very forthright in my dating profile and in my initial conversations with potential matches over just how much of a part the kids played in my life. I was also clear in stating that I was not looking to create a new family unit nor was I looking for a step-parent for the kids, since I felt and still do feel that the kids have two parents who love them and who are equally involved in their lives and upbringing such that there isn't a gap that *needs* filling. Whilst I was clear about starting off from this point, I was of course not mentally detaching myself from the logical conclusion that things could over time and in an ideal world develop such that things may ultimately end up in a new family unit being created, with us all moving in together and living happily ever after. The important distinction though is that this wasn't the motivation behind the endeavour but rather my motivation was to do something *for me*, to hopefully allow myself another go at finding a life-partner with whom to spend and share my life. I am unashamed about stating it in such a way that I know makes me sound quite selfish.

In reflecting upon this in terms of my dating and in the relationships that I have had, certainly more than 50% of relationships with single mothers have ultimately failed in part due to the other person not sharing this view or at least not to the same degree as me. This sounds over-simplistic and to an extent it probably is. I can reflect on all the relationships in question and point to various other aspects that weren't ideal for either me or the other person. However, the differences in our views in regard to the drivers for dating and the end-game that we were each considering was radically different and this ultimately undermined the future of things.

I am not sure exactly what to put this trend down to. I doubt that it is anything to do with me having been viewed by anyone I have dated as such a catch, that they could scarcely wait to get a ring on my finger (metaphorically speaking) and snare me for themselves. I speculate that to some degree this is possibly gender-related and at a fairly basic genetic level, driven by the mothering instinct to provide a safe and stable home for her and her child, in this instance by finding a mate who can fill a void and take care of them both. I am aware that this sounds in various degrees big-headed, chauvinistic and quite a leap of hypothesising. I am also keen to point out that in most instances I am talking about what were in fact relatively short relationships of on average 3 or so months. I would assume that the majority of the initial 'draw' for the women I dated was more in relation to the pursuit of fun and hopefully a bit of attraction rather than a carefully considered evaluation of whether I could shelter and provide for her and her offspring.

I would also emphasize that I have dated women with varying degrees of means and independence, ranging from career women who were in a far better state financially than me through to unemployed full-time mothers who had nothing materially to call their own and no aspiration other than to be a full-time mother. I can remember examples of the above behaviour that have been evidential in both extremes.

Fundamentally, I *do* believe this to be a factor for some women. It is something that is instinctive rather than calculating and which does contribute to how such women in this position behave (albeit subconsciously in most cases) in relatively new relationships.

This is the only way that I can explain how I, a man of modest financial means, with little in the way of small talk and at best a 6 out of 10 on the scale of looks, can have had experiences where:

a) one woman suggested she was willing to abandon her life and career to move in excess of 200 miles away from her extended family to move her and her child in with me in one example, or
b) another who offered to re-mortgage her house to assist me with clearing my personal debt after my separation as part of an amalgamation of our lives, a suggestion made mere months after we first went out together.

I certainly do not consider myself worthy of either of those things and for those reasons (and others) the relationships in question came to an end in due course.

The last impression that I want to give you about myself is that I am chauvinistic, judgemental or disdainful of the way that others conduct themselves (certainly not in the context of the examples cited above which were both heartfelt and flattering, not to mention undeserved towards me). I am repeatedly amazed, humbled and flattered by the generosity of the human spirit, and as a firm subscriber to trying to treat others as I wish to be treated, I am glad to say that I have for the most part been treated extremely well by those I have encountered in life, reciprocating how I have hopefully treated them.

My purpose in mentioning the above, as with many of the other things I have recounted in this book is to try and in some way make sense of my own experiences and to distil some of these into lessons that may be of assistance to you in your life. This is just one such observation that may have some root in established theories of human behaviour or it may just be utter speculation on my part. As I have experienced it, I include it and hope that you will take it at face value or ignore it depending on your mind-set.

As a final 'disclaimer' I would also emphasize that I think that the same motivations and behaviours could exist in reverse for a woman dating a single-father; in addition to being motivated to find a mate, the man could also be looking for someone to assist him as part of a joint-parenting team for the time when his kids are with him. This could be further motivated by him feeling that having a female by his side at some point in the future could enhance his life in a great many ways. The same motivators for seeking a new relationship could feasibly exist for both single-fathers and single-mothers alike and that regardless of gender, the single-parent in dating is undoubtedly evaluating not just the physical and mental attraction of the person they meet but also their suitability as a parent to their child.

Single person, with kids in their sole-care

The final type of person that I want to discuss is one closely linked to that described above; the single parent in the somewhat more complex situation whereby the kids have no contact with their other parent. I include this as a separate section since I believe that there are some subtle (and some not-so-subtle) differences that could arise in relation to your dating and potential future relationship with such a person.

I was never a particularly prolific dater, and certainly not someone who considered a date as an idle pastime (but instead has suffered the full gamut of dry-mouth, nervousness and general terror on each and every first date I've been on, and quite a lot of the second and third dates too). I can say through experience though that this is a circumstance that I have found exists in more than a handful of instances where I have met single mothers for dates.

There are lots of different circumstances that could pertain to both Mums and Dads that could have led to the situation whereby they are single-parents and their kids do not have any contact with the other parent. They could be widowed, or there could be severe medical issues relating to one parent's mental or physical health that may render them unable to be a parent. There may have been some sort of legal intervention either as a result of the parting of the relationship or subsequently which forcibly prevents the other parent from having anything to do with the child for reasons such as a history of violence or abuse towards either the child or the parent. Alternatively, and sadly considering what is at stake it can also arise on the whim of the parent who maintains custody and refuses to let the other parent have any access (the other parent may or may not have the means, inclination or resolve to contest this and pursue it through legal channels). Finally, the other parent may just have disappeared and actually does not even want to be involved which is unfortunately also fairly common in my experience.

I have dated women who have accounted for many of these different scenarios (I am pleased to say that I have never met a widow of an age that I would have dated them, and say 'pleased' since for this circumstance to arise would certainly have meant the untimely death of some poor guy at a tragically young age).

In the instance of the example where the other parent was unable to play a part in their child's life due to suffering severely from epilepsy and seizures, this must have been an extremely challenging situation for all involved. The relationship in between the child's parents hadn't failed because of these seizures. The net effect though was that with the child residing with its mother, there was little scope for them to spend more than an hour or so with its father and certainly never unsupervised. This was due to the ever-impending threat of a seizure that could render the father unable to care for or even be responsible for the child; a tragic scenario indeed.

In the second instance, the father had been subject of a court order preventing him access to the child and had also been placed on the sex-offenders register for inappropriate behaviour with a child relative of the woman I was dating. In this extremely unfortunate circumstance, it was morally and legally impossible for the father to have any contact with his son and as such there was no visitation and no mention of the guy in the lives of the woman or her child, quite rightly and understandably.

In the final instance I dated a woman who had a child a few years younger than my youngest daughter. This relationship was certainly one of the most serious and enduring that I have entered into since parting from my ex-wife (more on this later). In the context of this chapter the relevant elements of this experience were as follows; whilst she initially had an informally agreed access arrangement with the father of their child, at some point she took issue with his conduct, his parenting-style and the lack of support that she perceived that she received from him. Without warning she then decided to withdraw his access rights to their son, moved their son to a different school without informing the father, and moved house and would not inform the child's father as to where they now resided. I am not proud of the part that I played in tolerating and in conceptually supporting this course of events but feel it is important to relay in the context of this chapter to illustrate the point. The key thing was that at this point in the relationship and subsequently for a period of months the child had no involvement with his father, in this case pretty-much solely due to a whim on the part of the mother.

Such scenarios are unfortunately all too common and implemented on the sole basis of whatever justification is provided by the parent withdrawing the access rights of the other parent. These informal arrangements seem to be established and enforced with the custodial parent as judge, jury and executioner, acting with autonomy, impunity and without regard for whether their actions are justified or fair to all parties, least of all the kids. It is then up to the other parent to contest this through official channels which can undoubtedly be a lengthy, costly, time-consuming and unrewarding process in itself. The effects are deep, wide and far-reaching on all involved.

Returning to consideration of the possibilities of building a relationship with such a person in general terms, it is obvious that the challenges faced in a relationship with a person who has sole-custody of the kids are very similar to those where custody is shared. The immediate and obvious differences are in relation to there being little or no time available to the person for dating or to invest themselves in the new relationship except where special arrangements are made for the child's care. This is unfortunate, but realistically it places enormous barriers in the way of getting a relationship underway in the first instance and also makes it extremely difficult for the relationship to develop if it were already underway, based on my experience.

That is certainly not to say that this makes it impossible nor anything but a worthwhile challenge to overcome for both of you. However, there is no question over how much more difficult it will be in order for the person to find the time to service their own need for space and time to devote to their own happiness outside of being a parent. This must unfortunately be a challenge that such parents have in many other aspects of their life too.

What compounds this situation further is that it seems to me that it is the full-time single parent who most needs or at least would most-value the opportunity to have some time that is focussed upon doing something for themselves to enrich their lives aside from being a parent. They need to devote attention to meeting their own needs and doing something for their own enjoyment (such as dating and exploring the possibility of meeting someone else with whom to spend some time), and yet the paradox is that these are the individuals who have the least time to do so.

I am certainly not in possession of any answers that will assist such people in overcoming this. What I am grateful for is that this is not a circumstance that I have had to deal with personally but it emphasizes to me yet another of the positive side effects of shared-parenting that I have a good amount of time to devote to myself, to dating and to the pursuit of a new relationship.

Lessons learned in the pursuit of love

I have attempted to draw some lessons and generalisations based on the experiences I have had with regard to the types of people I have encountered through dating, above. I have tried to organise these lessons so that they are to some degree applicable to both Mums and Dads in shared-parenting arrangements and I believe that to a greater or lesser degree, the same types will be encountered whether you are looking to date men or women.

Aside from these lessons, I would like to present below a summary of some of the other key things I have learned in my time in dating. I present these with my tongue slightly in cheek at times, and with a caveat that I am not someone whose guidance you should rely upon as gospel in such matters; A divorcee male at the age of 40 with numerous failed relationships in his wake is unlikely to be credible as an expert in the field of dating. However I would hope that some of my lessons may be of use, or at least amusement!

I believe that the following are worthy of consideration by anyone with kids who may be embarking on dating following the breakdown of their relationship. These lessons pertain to both online dating, and the 'old-school' method of chatting someone up in a bar/nightclub/supermarket/post office queue (although some are more applicable to online dating only). For simplicity, I have used the terms 'online' and 'old-school' to differentiate these. Let's dive straight in.

Lesson 1 – There is no point in being passive about your activities to elicit a date. If you are using an online dating site then you should approach people you like the look of, send winks, nudges or whatever your site of choice allows you to do; but preferably send an email or a communication of some substance. Similarly, in the old-school world there is nothing better than actually approaching someone you like the look of, smiling, saying hello and striking up conversation. The thought of this may fill you with fear and terror in either scenario (primarily through the inherent fear of rejection or rebuttal of your efforts). There is unfortunately an element of this being a numbers-game and it is far better to put yourself out there and give yourself a chance of establishing the dialogue that may lead somewhere, than vainly hoping that you will get results through just presenting yourself to your market (through putting up an online profile or hanging around in a bar looking amazing). Of course both these preliminary steps will help too, but what I am saying is don't expect these to be enough.

Lesson 2 – Invest yourself in the process of getting yourself a date. I am a firm believer in the old adage that 'if a job is worth doing, it is worth doing well'. The application of this cliché to the world of dating is that fundamentally there is little point in making a half-hearted job of trying to find yourself a date and expecting this to yield the results that you want it to. When you consider all that is at stake (quite conceivably you are looking to meet the person with whom you hope you will strike up a happy and fulfilling relationship) why on earth would you approach this with any less than 100% effort and commitment? I am not saying that this should become your primary focus in life since we all have jobs to hold down, kids to raise, bills to pay and so on. However, this endeavour is equally worthy of your attention and efforts as exercising, keeping your home in order, getting enough sleep and eating healthily. It is possible to devote 100% commitment to everything that you do without any one thing coming at the expense of the other. Specific to each of the 'types' of dating:

- If you are going to use online dating then invest some time in your online profile. Make sure that even if you don't write much, that it is considered, honest, clear and thorough and gives the reader some insight into who you are. That you have put in some effort and done more than the ubiquitous "I like crazy nights out and also a takeaway and a DVD at home on the couch" will score you points with anyone who is worth your attention.

- Ensure that you have at least one good, recent picture of yourself on your profile. It is obvious (or maybe not given how often this is ignored) but if you have no picture, then the message that is sub-consciously sent out is that you have something to hide. I believe it is equally pointless to put up a picture that is 5 years old and which represents you looking at your best (in your own mind). Be proud of who you are, what you look like, and confident in your appearance. In the age of digital photography, it takes little time and effort to have a friend take a few hundred pictures of you and to pick the one that you are happiest with.

- The same rationale applies to the consideration that you should give to the emails you are sending when approaching people. I accept that with this being a numbers game to some degree, it would be frustrating and time-consuming to compose each and every email with content specifically tailored to the person you are contacting. I'd suggest a light and cheery opener mentioning at least one thing that demonstrates that you have read their profile and a desire to open a conversation if they are interested in your profile, as a bare minimum. Anything more (or less) than this, up to an including your favourite joke, a 'text speak' message of about 9 characters, or a request to know their surname so you can start practicing your married signature are best avoided in my view. The time-consuming bit can be avoided for the most part by copying and pasting. Get creative!
- If you are going down the old-school route, adopt the mind-set of someone who is open, warm and friendly when you are out in the world. I'm not suggesting that you become someone who is permanently on the prowl for love, evaluating everyone they encounter as a possible match, and flirting with everyone they meet. However, it is essential to carry yourself as someone who is reasonably confident, happy in themselves, open, approachable and above all, who smiles in a natural and warm way. I know that this is easy to say and potentially challenging to do, but if you are not all of those things already, then I would suggest that these should be your goal first and foremost before pursuing dates. There is nothing more essential as a pre-requisite for life generally, or for pursuing a relationship specifically than to be happy in your own skin and secure in who you are. These two traits usually shine-through in a person's character and are extremely attractive to others too.

Lesson 3 – Invest time in yourself to make you feel and look better. I am careful not to stray into the territory where this book becomes the catch-all self-help manual of our time. However as someone who in the time since the breakdown of my marriage has seen their weight and fitness levels fluctuate from what, on an online dating site would be classed as 'Big and Beautiful' to the classification 'Athletic and Toned' I feel that I am in a pretty good position to talk about the enormous benefits that can be reaped from being able to honestly class yourself as the latter.

This is not a call to arms for everyone to immediately ditch the carbs and head to the gym for the sake of it but the spirit of this lesson if any, is that we all know deep down that when we look good, we feel good. It is good to do the right things for our health for the benefits that this gives us alone, however there can be no doubt that when we are actively exercising a little bit more, eating a little more healthily, drinking a little bit less alcohol and are not smoking (or at least smoking less) then we *do* all feel better in ourselves. This then naturally reflects in our outer appearance and in the sense of calm, happiness and wellbeing that shines through in the way we look and the way we behave.

I cannot tell you to undertake a particular programme of diet or exercise as I am not qualified to, and in any case there are numerous other books available that do this. What I would say though is that no matter who you are, we all have the scope to make little changes in our lives that will pay enormous dividends in the improvements that are yielded for our heath, wellbeing and appearance. Try it today; the next time you are contemplating whether you need another glass of wine, a banana or a chocolate bar, whether to walk or drive to the shop, or whether you really want a cigarette that has been offered to you, try making the right decision in any of those instances and see how good that feels. Start making those right decisions more times than you choose the wrong things, start 'winning more battles' and watch the results spiral. Honestly, it works. And in the context of dating, this will manifest itself in you being a happier and more contented person when on dates, and I guarantee more attractive physically and spiritually as well.

Lesson 4 – Be true to who you are and what you want. This is definitely a lesson learned over time, and something that really only comes with experience. I say this on the basis that I think that it would be a rare person who sets out in adult life with a refined list of the things they want in a future partner from the outset. I firmly believe that you cannot know until you experience life a little. When we part from a long-term relationship that has been (presumably) serious and loving, there will be some learning points that we take forward about what traits, behaviours and characteristics we value and things which that we must absolutely avoid in a future mate. Our wish list will be shaped by all our life experiences rather than merely 'someone who is nothing like my ex'! The list of things you want and don't want in a future partner, and how you wish to be treated will no doubt grow and become clearer to you as you develop more life experience. I believe it is crucial that you are true to this and strive to achieve it in your search for a new partner.

You should not be unwilling to compromise on things since I think that the fundamental basis of a healthy relationship is the ability to compromise, to put the other person's needs first, and to feel confident that they treat you equally and in the same way. It is essential to feel assured of who you are and what you want and furthermore to stand by your list when you are dating and meeting others who you might consider as a future partner.

Such a list could contain anything from a person's hair-colour or profession, through to whether they practice a religion or whether they support a local football team. But it should also consider aspects such as whether you are willing to date someone who has children (or wants children), what part their extended family plays in their life, whether they are sociable or introverted, or any other facet that could influence how you get on with them.

The key is to identify the things that are *absolutely essential* to you and to then stick to your guns. Don't get distracted or flattered by advances from people who do not meet these essential criteria just because you are lonely, or compromise on things that will ultimately make you unhappy if not fulfilled. Your happiness is at stake. The happiness of your kids also hinges on this. The happiness of the other people is also an important factor too; treat others as you wish to be treated, remember?

Lesson 5 – Take it at your own pace, but beware of excessive caution. This lesson is primarily derived from my experiences in online dating but I believe that it could pertain equally to the 'old-school' camp. Over time, the typical route for online dating liaisons has typically proven to be: Initial wink/nudge/email followed by a reply (probably a little flirtatious to establish genuine rapport/interest) followed by an email dialogue of increasingly lengthy emails 'within' the site. This will be followed at some point by moving the email dialogue to 'proper' email addresses so that further photos can be exchanged. I believe that the same general course of action is likely for an initial 'old-school' meeting where inevitably email addresses or mobile phone numbers will be exchanged to facilitate further conversation. The point is that it can be possible to get drawn into an exchange that is more akin to being pen-pals or correspondents rather than two people wishing to get to know each other better and establish if there is the prospect of a more serious relationship beyond the initial attraction.

I accept that there is a need to develop some familiarity and to get a bit more comfortable with the person you have met (in either the real or the virtual world) to ensure that they meet your essential criteria as a potential match (and that they aren't a prospective serial killer, amongst other things). There does come a point though where you risk running out of things to talk about before you've even met. I have known situations where I've ended up feeling like I know pretty much everything there is to know about a lady from her earliest childhood memory to her favourite flavour of ice-cream before we've even met in person. Whilst this can be a positive thing to some degree in that you can establish with a reasonable degree of certainty that you are likely to get on and that you have lots in common I believe there is also a very real danger a) that when you meet up in person for the first time, you have little in the way of small talk to offer or conversely that b) you almost feel compelled or obliged to enter into a relationship of sorts merely on the basis that you have effectively pre-committed yourself to the person through the time you have invested.

This investment of time and the fact that you have basically convinced yourself that you like and get on with them before you ever meet in person can blind you to the other factors that might otherwise have also been considerations. Put bluntly you might find them to be unattractive in person compared to their pictures, they may be a dominant conversationalist where you prefer someone who listens to you, or they may offer crushing anecdotes and be one of those people who always has to out-do others in conversation, or any number of other things that can't necessarily be established until you meet. All these are things that might have been considered at face value more if you hadn't invested so much time up-front in getting to know them, via email where many (if not all) of these facets can be overlooked or hidden.

I suggest that once you have established that you are probably okay with this person, that they meet your essential criteria based on what you know and you are convinced that they don't pose a threat to your personal safety, then why not consider suggesting meeting up in person. This may just save you a bit of time in weeding out those who are a good 10 years older, 6 inches shorter or 30 pounds heavier than they said they were. It may enable the early exposure of other character or personality defects that they are trying to keep hidden. Positively speaking, it may just mean that you get to know them better, quicker than you might have done and that you get entrenched in a positive relationship all the sooner.

Lesson 6 – Don't commit yourself too quickly. This is my equivalent of 'playing it cool' or 'playing hard to get'. I would rather think of it as a means of not losing sight of yourself and your needs and not submitting yourself too quickly into the role of being part of a relationship, rather than showing a lack of commitment out of a desire to be stand-offish.

It took me a long while before I came to the realisation that what I was typically doing when I met someone new and started dating them was that I was quickly throwing myself into things wholeheartedly and failing to protect my own time, space and interests as I became more and more embroiled in the relationship in the early weeks and months. I am not suggesting that you shouldn't be enthusiastic at the start of a relationship or that you wouldn't naturally want to spend time with the new person in your life when your parenting commitments allow. Nor am I suggesting that one should be either evasive or protectionist about your time and space. However I think that a balance does need to be struck between enthusiastically entering into a new relationship whilst also maintaining the things, activities and people that were in your life previously. Examples of this could include neglecting or excessively reducing the amount of time that you spend with friends in sporting or leisure pursuits or even just in catching up with them in favour of seeing your new love-interest, reducing the amount of time you spend exercising to get free time back or even worse, as you feel like you've done the hard bit in winning someone's affection and you can now let yourself go! You may perhaps find yourself bending and modifying forthcoming arrangements or making long-term future plans with them (such as buying concert tickets together or planning holidays months ahead).

All of the above examples are things that I have been guilty of; I've blown-out friends and cancelled plans I had previously made to accommodate the person I was dating, I have reduced my exercise to accommodate them, and in one instance I bought flight tickets for them to take part in a family holiday that was months ahead (by the time the holiday came round we were long-since finished). The point that I am trying to illustrate is that whilst I am encouraging you generally to take action and positive pro-active steps towards finding people to date, once you have found someone you are keen on it is far healthier to let things proceed at a steady and measured pace rather than feeling that you must charge headlong into a full-on relationship where there is some obliged commitment of 100% of your free time. This can serve to ensure that either the other person is scared away by the intensity of your approach or that you quickly burn-out having expended every scrap of your time, energy and possibly also money on a new relationship. It is likely that it was really only in its formative phase and which probably realistically needed the passage of time to determine if it was going to succeed or fail regardless of what happened or how much you put into it.

Most importantly of all though, taking the above radical steps demonstrates that as an individual you are failing to do the most important thing which is to take care of yourself and to look after your own interests and the very many facets of you, first and foremost. We all need to love and be loved and the pursuit of a relationship to find this is an admirable cause. However, we also each need to take care of our health and physical, mental and emotional wellbeing through exercise, leisure pursuits and through time spent alone and with friends and family. To neglect these aspects of our lives will only be detrimental to ourselves and will harm our relationships with friends and family as well. Furthermore, this has a very real potential to knock-on to the quality of our parenting to our kids since it affects our overall outlook and our ability to fulfil this crucial role. I speak from experience on this.

Lesson 7 – Be wary of how soon to introduce them to your kids. This is probably the 'Golden Rule' in terms of dating and its effects and possible impacts on your shared-parenting arrangement. The obvious question eventually comes around at some point after you have met someone, established that there exists the attraction, the chemistry and a mutual desire to continue to see each other and see where things go; 'when would it be good for them to meet my kids?'

This is prompted by a number of factors. Presumably you have found someone who you think may stand a chance of becoming a long-standing fixture in your life and you feel that the time is right for them to meet the little people who are already a permanent fixture in your life. This is a positive show of commitment on behalf of a single parent as they start dating someone, and is possibly one of the most serious steps we can take. It is a statement of commitment that is based around opening up not just your own vulnerability but that of the kids who rely on you and who trust your judgement since you are one of the main gatekeepers of those who come into their lives. It is also a gesture endowed with an enormous amount of implied trust. To the other person, whether they have kids of their own to reciprocate with or not it must also come as a significant move and possibly also something that is more than a little scary.

There will be a number of things to consider in regard to the decision as to whether to make the introduction. Being someone who thinks in terms of lists let me summarise it as follows:

1) **Based on the maturity, adaptability and general confidence of your kids do you feel that they will be able to understand who this person is and what the significance of their introduction is?** Presumably the main purpose of the introduction should be to allow you to spend more time with the person when you have your kids with you, but certainly initially this hopefully isn't solely intended as a means to allow you to have that person stay over in your home, nor is it pursuit of a licence to spend your time kissing and cuddling in front of your kids. In theory then it shouldn't be something that has any greater magnitude as far as the child is concerned than for them to meet one of your friends? Consider the motive and what you are looking to get out of it since this could either mean you are making a big deal out of nothing, or alternatively that you are making the introduction purely for selfish motives on your part (remember Golden Rule #1 still applies at all times!) If this is the case, then perhaps you should reassess your plans?

2) **How do you feel about the person? Are you really sure that this is the time to introduce them to your kids?** This check-point in the new relationship in your life is often a useful point to stand back and assess whether you are really doing this because it feels like the right thing to do. This consideration will be based largely on whether you feel like the relationship is going somewhere and you can see a future for yourself with

this person or whether in actual fact it just seems like the right thing to do because you've spent a number of weeks or months dating them and can't put it off any longer. I can look back on a few instances where I was swept-along with the momentum of the new relationship. If I had really taken the opportunity to analyse how I felt about the decision to introduce the person to my kids based on how I felt about where the relationship was going, it might well have lead me to question whether I really saw a future in it. Instead I think I genuinely got in a rather formulaic pattern whereby after a couple of months with the person, it felt like the commitment and future longevity of the relationship was implied and so I never really questioned the introducing of the person to my kids. Still, we live and learn.

3) **What has been your kids' experience of adapting to new people coming into your life (and that of your ex)?** Based on their age and how much time has elapsed since you parted from your ex there will likely have been at least one person who has come into the kids' lives, introduced as either Mum's or Dad's new boyfriend or girlfriend (and I don't rule out at this point that either could apply to both Mum and Dad, although I don't intend to broach the subject of marriages parting to allow for the development of same-sex relationships since I don't have any first-hand experience to offer in this regard myself; albeit that I have known at least one example where it happened in my social network). Chances are that the kids will have met someone badged as such either through you or through your ex, and it is more than likely that this person (or people) will also have at some point ceased to be involved with the kids as the relationship fails. I hold a couple of conflicting views on the possible effects of this type of change on kids views of the world, and these views are shaped purely by my own observations regarding my kids.

In the 10 or so years (at time of writing) that I have been apart from my ex, there have been a number of people that either she or I have introduced to the kids as either our new partners/boyfriends/girlfriends or as the kids have got older, more subtly as people who we are dating. We have also each been engaged once since then but each broke this off before the second marriage ensued in both our cases. Our new partners moved in with us in both of these instances. I thoroughly regret that a number of these people ever met the kids, not due to them being a negative influence on the kids or because they were ever anything other than kind and positive towards the kids, but in fact for this very reason. It must be tough as a child to have people coming into and out of your life who are identified to you as a person of some significance (by which I mean more than a friend or acquaintance), for them to treat you well and for them then to subsequently cease to be a feature in your life. Our kids develop a sense of adaptability in regard to such change and this starts from the point at which their parents part. They inevitably have to get used to the fact that people do come and go into and out of relationships and it is a reality of life that this happens. Whilst it is easier as an adult to rationalise this knowing that there are always reasons why relationships fail, as a child the last thing that you probably want having allowed yourself to trust a new person or at least to feel at-ease around them, is to hear that you are not going to see them again.

The flip-side of this same view for me also holds some weight in as much as I think that the lessons it teaches kids can be valuable to them. Certainly, as I have stated before you are the model for your child's view on relationships and it is through you that they learn how relationships work, that you have to work at them in order to get the best out of them, and that you shouldn't accept or just put up with a relationship that is not giving you what you want, need or deserve. Therefore, and *with careful consideration and sensitive handling* it can be helpful to your kids learning that relationships fail and why, provided that you communicate with them in terms they understand the reasons why your relationship with person-x failed, and why the kids won't see them again. I also firmly believe that the communication that this approach can encourage between you and your child is useful in allowing the discussion of some aspects of human relationships that might not otherwise come up for them in a traditional family setting. To be clear, I am certainly not saying that you should go out and deliberately pursue relationships, introduce the person to your kids and then dump them just so you can teach your kids a lesson about life! What I am saying though is that you can make sure that you don't just bring people into your kids' lives, then remove them thus eroding their faith in relationships or their ability to trust that new people won't just abandon them, by ensuring that you encourage open and honest conversations with your kids along the way to help them understand better what has happened.

The final thing that I want to mention in this regard is probably related to the age of my kids and the fact that they have had 10 years to mature within the context of our shared-parenting arrangement. The fundamental point is that my kids often voiced that they wanted me to find a new girlfriend (bizarrely in something of a role-reversal) since they worried about me being lonely! I am willing to accept that this is a measure of the maturity and adaptability of my kids as well as a factor no doubt due to their advanced years. I also think that this demonstrates that through adopting an open communication with my kids through the years since I parted from their Mum (in relation to all aspects of life, not just my relationships) it has enabled them to understand that this is a complex aspect of our lives but one that also plays a part in their happiness too. I believe that as a result of this experience they have a heightened understanding of what adult relationships are all about. Of course they also venture views and opinions in the matter that can be at once amusing and also insightful; my eldest daughter once ventured that if I bought a cooler car, it might assist me in getting a girlfriend; valuable and treasured advice!

Lesson 8 – Consider how to introduce the person to your kids. This is definitely one of the more loosely defined lessons since there are a number of variables and 'it all depends' considerations to be made. One of the main things to weigh up after agreeing timing is how much of a big deal to make of it. I have experienced scenarios both where a casual meeting in passing, with the kids in tow was how I introduced them to the new lady and other events of greater magnitude (such as going to a sporting event) so that the event was the main focal point and the kids got to take their time in getting to know the new person. I think that either can be workable and successful if the right approach is taken. Critical success factors for me in this regard would be:

- To not place any burden of expectation on either your kid's part or those of the person you are introducing for everyone to get on. Naturally you would hope that the adults in the situation would make the effort to bridge the gap but there should be no need to force anyone to be any more outgoing or effervescent that they would naturally be.
- To not force any uncomfortable situations for anyone, most of all the kids (such as leaving the kids alone with the person so that anyone feels pressure to get on).

- To not make the visit/activity/meeting too long. Such events can be quite intense when everyone is on their 'best-behaviour' and as such a relatively brief encounter that leaves everyone wanting more is far preferable to a monumental meeting that goes on and on
- To not expect the kids to be on their best behaviour or to get stressed when this inevitably doesn't materialise. The situation is likely to be somewhat stressful for all, and potentially confusing and a little disconcerting for your kids to some degree regardless of their age, so don't be surprised when this gives rise to acting up for your attention, shyness or even a tantrum. This is important so as not to *force* your child to have to comply, but also it will give the person you are introducing to them a realistic picture of what your kids (and all kids!) are like. There is no point in trying to portray a sedate, harmonious and utopian view of family life merely to win the person round; realism is the order of the day!

The other facet of the introduction to your kids is to consider how to approach it when you both have kids. The main consideration here is around whether to do the introductions one family at a time, or to throw everyone into one introduction. Both have their individual merits, one perhaps in softening the blow for everyone, and giving each adult the opportunity to gradually bond with the other person's kids. The flip-side is that when you get all the kids together in one meeting, it probably assists in shifting the focus from the adults onto the kids, and making it more of a play-date where there just happen to be other adults there too. I have experienced both, and can say conclusively that there are merits to both approaches. On the whole though the latter has seemed to work better, since come the end, the kids are usually keen to know when they can see person-x's kids again.

As I mentioned at the top of the chapter, I want to constrain this chapter to matters of dating as they relate to shared-parenting and that is what I have attempted to do with the above rules. I could go on to considerations regarding whether you should go on a first date on a weekend, or who should pay for the first date through to what to do if the other person requests your mobile number before you've even met. However, I will save those lessons, and the salutary tales that gave rise to them for another book once I have time to write them down!

Being true to yourself and what you want

One thing that I want to come back to is related to Lesson 4 above, and I want to discuss it a little more thoroughly. I don't consider myself to be particularly hung-up on having a type. I have historically been in relationships with more brunettes than blondes and have dated career-women, full-time mothers, fitness fanatics and those whose main exercise was a night out dancing in a club, punctuated by the occasional cigarette break. One of the main considerations through my dating life (and which probably influenced the content at the top of this chapter) has always been the question over how I felt regarding whether the woman I was dating had kids or not.

I had very few points of reference for dating prior to meeting Jo since I was someone who always seemed to be friends with girls rather than managing to secure myself a girlfriend with any regularity or success. When she and I parted and I eventually undertook to get back into dating and my first relationship (of little more than a few months) was with someone who had a child of a similar age to my youngest. When the initial flush of enthusiasm and excitement over the new relationship had faded, there emerged a number of points of concern ranging from minor annoyances to significant personality clashes that meant in my mind that the relationship was doomed to fail. However, one of the main issues that I had with the whole set-up which had undoubtedly been nagging at me from the start was that I wasn't particularly happy being with someone who had their own child, at that time in my life. I had no issue with the child, and was already realistic at this point that possible matches would be more likely to have kids already in order that they were contemplating dating single-dad. My difficulties stemmed from the fact that I felt extremely guilty (more on this later) over the fact that I was spending time with someone else's child when I couldn't spend as much time as I would like to have been able to with my own kids.

When the relationship inevitably came to swift end shortly after, I resolved that the next person I would date would have to not have kids on this basis. Whilst I stuck to my guns in this, it highlighted to me the other points that I had mentioned above regarding the potential hazards/issues in dating someone who doesn't have kids and you do; namely that they can struggle to accept and adapt to the time and resource required to accommodate the kids, and that they may not necessarily be the most comfortable in interacting with kids.

Based on my growing experience and the more or less constant thoughts that ran through my head regarding how to get what I wanted (and more importantly, *what I actually wanted*) I came to the realisation that what I needed was someone who had their own kids, but who wasn't actually looking for someone to play a central part in their kid's lives and wasn't overly bothered about playing a part in the lives of mine.

This too was a massively artificial circumstance to imagine since the conclusion would be that with time, if things were progressing healthily then at some point there would be a reasonable need and desire to become more entrenched in each other's lives and interact with each other's kids. Besides, what was clear was that I really needed to get my own views straight in regard to dealing with the guilt that I felt when spending time with others' kids. This was something that I found abated over time anyway, but was also resolved through counselling that I undertook to discuss and resolve this and some other issues that were left in my mind following the breakdown of my marriage.

The final child-related element that I battled with for a considerable period of time was over the question of whether I would ever enter into the idea of having more kids with a potential future match. In the early days after my parting from Jo I was honestly unsure about this. Since my entry to the world of parenthood had not been made in a particularly planned or considered way, it was something of a foreign concept to me that one could enter into parenthood willingly! Our second child had been conceived and born in wedlock, but I am pretty sure that at the time this felt like the natural thing to do, in that we were newly married and already had one child so the time had come to bring about a sibling. I contend that this is not the same as contemplating another child, with different parenting to my existing kids. I view this as a much bigger consideration which would have to be evaluated in the context of the existing life I had with my new partner and whether I felt completely stable and secure in that. I couldn't contemplate entering into a situation where I could end up trying to service two shared-parenting arrangements if things ever went awry again!

As time has passed and my kids have got older we are now able to do more in the way of activities that we all enjoy together, have conversations that challenge and interest us all and generally do things that I was always excited about doing with my kids just as I had enjoyed doing things with my parents; I'm sure that it is possible for parent and child alike to enjoy a trip to the soft-play centre when they are little but I am more about playing sports with my kids or taking them to a movie at the cinema that we are all actually interested in watching! With this in mind I have become more certain than ever that I do not wish to have further kids in any relationship. I always placated my inner demons in my early twenties when my contemporaries were still partying and enjoying greater financial means than had been available as students at University, and I was learning how to change nappies and dispensing night-time feeds, that at least when my kids were of an age to leave home as independent adults I would still be under the age of 50. This has remained a motivating factor for me and I'm sorry if you think me selfish for saying so.

To this end, my 'mission statement' if you want to refer to it as such has been to meet someone:

- who may or may not have kids
- who has established parenting arrangements in place with their ex and who will be able to enjoy and interact with my own kids
- who has similar expectations in regard to my interaction with their kids
- who does not want to have any further kids

I have staunchly stuck to this criteria since having the realisation that this was the most important factor in considering the suitability of a future match (alongside the physical and mental attraction, and chemistry of course).

This is not a formula for everyone else, but is provided to illustrate what I mean in terms of knowing what you want. It is of absolute and fundamental importance for a person to know themselves and to understand what makes them tick, and furthermore to know exactly what they want and need out of a future match. It is also absolutely pivotal for them to stick to this wish-list staunchly when pursuing a future partner.

I say this with absolute conviction, since I learned the hardest way possible the dangers that not doing this can give rise to, through my part in the failing of the only long-term and enduring relationship that I have entered into since parting from my wife. It is the lessons of this relationship which I will discuss in the context of my shared-parenting arrangement in the next chapter.

Chapter 10 – Moving on

This chapter is about the further lessons and experiences I have gained while moving forward with life, in particular with reference to the process of trying to integrate my family with another. This came about as a result of my getting engaged to someone who had a child in her own parenting arrangement with her child's father. I will state at the outset that ultimately this relationship failed for a variety of reasons (some of which I will touch upon in this chapter). The main purpose of including this account is not so much to discuss what went wrong and whose fault it was but to highlight the lessons that I have taken from this experience with particular reference to shared-parenting.

It is okay to be good to yourself

The overall themes of this chapter bring to mind Golden Rule #4, and why it is so important.

> *Golden Rule #4* – Once Golden Rule #1 has been satisfied, it is okay for the shared-parenting arrangement to be designed for the mutual and individual benefit of the parents. Ensure though that it is equally beneficial otherwise resentments and negativity will creep in.

I mention this again since it resonates with my view that all too often single-parents shackle themselves with guilt over the effects that they have brought about for their kids in parting from their ex. They convince themselves that somehow a deserved-penitence is for them to never again consider their own wants, needs and desires in life since the sole focus of their lives should be their kids.

I hope by now that you understand that the Golden Rules that I suggest within this book for the establishment of shared-parenting are not things that I believe you can pick and choose from, but that all need to be applied in balance to make it work. Equal in importance and significance within these is the Golden Rule above that says it is okay for you to make the shared-parenting arrangement to work for you as an individual and as a parent, as well as it working for your kids. My fundamental belief is that if I am in myself happy, fulfilled and contented with all aspects of my life then this will only enhance the ability with which I serve my kids as their father.

I have the relatively intense demands of being the single-parent during the weeks they live with me where I have to fulfil the roles that in a normal family would be split between Mum and Dad, on my own and without support. I consider myself very lucky that I also have the time when they are with their Mum to re-charge, re-group and reflect, but also time that is solely based around taking care of myself and my needs.

Of course my parenting responsibility, instinct and my love and concern for my kids doesn't go away at these times and indeed I will often see them either for a visit, in passing or at some sporting club or event when they are at on a week at their Mums. Thanks to my eldest daughters hearty-embracing of the miracles of text messaging, am seldom out of contact with them anyway. However, I am unashamed in the fact that I have allowed and even encouraged myself to embrace the times when I don't have the kids as *my time*.

I am reluctant for you to think of this time as purely self-indulgent, self-centred and a non-stop rollercoaster of fun, frolics and good times. Within these periods I ensure I use the time to maximise my exercise-time, I do the majority of my housework and food shopping, I catch up on personal administration and work that I have perhaps not been able to catch up on when the kids were with me and I earmark time to attempt the DIY projects that I know would be best accomplished when the kids aren't trying to 'help'. I also use this time to plan activities with friends, arrange dates, go to gigs and concerts, visit friends and relatives for weekends, play my music loud and watch the news on the TV in the lounge rather than relegating myself to the kitchen or bedroom. I cook the food that I want to eat, when I want it and generally indulge myself in all the things that I either cannot do when the kids are around or which would at least be more difficult or require a babysitter or other special arrangements to enable.

It is a simple and obvious point that it is easier to please yourself in non-kids weeks than in weeks when you have them with you. I genuinely believe though that the mind-set of not just accepting or doing it, but in actually embracing the opportunity and feeling good about yourself in doing so is an essential mental shift to make. This ensures that you function effectively and to the best of your ability in your shared-parenting arrangement when the kids are in your care. Such a shift will ensure that you are the best person you can be for your own benefit, and for the benefit of your kids.

It is okay to move on
Taking the concept above further, I am aware that many single parents struggle with the notion of allowing themselves to even contemplate, never mind to actually pursue the idea of finding a new partner or even to go on a few dates with someone else. This can be for a variety of reasons. It may include the preservation of some loyalty to their ex or residual pain from their split (especially prevalent I think where there has been some infidelity on one or other persons part in the failing of their relationship) which makes it difficult for them to entertain the idea of moving on. In the instance where they were cheated-on in the course of their marriage it may be that they feel like their ex executed the ultimate betrayal of trust towards

their marriage, and that for them to move on and date someone else may on some subconscious level be a similar betrayal to the sanctity of their marriage or relationship. Alternatively, in the instance whereby the person had been the individual who cheated on their spouse, they may be so wracked with guilt over the consequences of their original betrayal, which ultimately led to the relationship splitting up, that they struggle to allow themselves to commit to any new relationship. These are only personal theories and have no basis other than my own speculation and observations on those I have met; however, I feel that both instances can play a part in a single-parent struggling to move on.

The same effect could also arise for single-parents for other reasons. Factors such as guilt for devoting time, resource, money or energy (physical or mental) to anything other than sustaining life for you and your kids can be of enormous significance in the early weeks and months following a split (I look more closely at guilt in another chapter since I believe it is an enormously significant factor in much of shared-parenting and life in general).

Similarly, the time and efforts that it can also demand to just keep things ticking-over when you are suddenly thrown into the world of single-parenting are all-consuming. It is not to be under-estimated just how little one can feel is left in the metaphorical tank to do anything other than just get through life when you are dealing with the daily rigours of parenting.

Without speculating further on reasons that a single-parent could feel reluctant to allow themselves to move forward with life (many of the above have at some point been the case for me, I should add), at some point with the passing of time we will usually reach the conclusion that actually yes, life does go on. You want to enjoy the one attempt you get at life and for many/most this will involve finding a new someone to enjoy it with.

I have already provided quite an extensive summary of the lessons gleaned from my years of dating following the parting from my ex. If little of this is relevant or interesting to others then what I hope it does at least affirm is that I have some years of experience to talk about which further emphasizes the lengths I have gone to in order to find that special someone.

At one point a few years after embarking upon shared-parenting I genuinely thought that I had found that person, and following years of beating myself up internally for the path of my life and the guilt that I had harboured following the split from my ex, it seemed like the stars were aligned that in finally having worked through these issues I had met someone with whom I felt might be my partner for life.

The details of the account below are based on a phase of my life that I now look back on as one of the most eventful and emotional. It encompasses some of the highest highs and the lowest lows that I have ever experienced, and it has only been as a result of the passing of time that I feel I can objectively look back on it now and draw out the lessons learned.

The relationship came about through the by-now tried and trusted channel of online dating. The details of our meeting and getting to know each other followed a fairly standard pattern that contributed to the lessons I've documented above regarding my experiences in dating. The pertinent facts were that we seemed to share similar outlooks, value-systems, interests and both had kids. The crucial difference was that she didn't have a particularly amicable relationship with the father of her kids which was in stark contrast to the shared-parenting arrangement that I had for mine.

As time passed we became closer and spent much more time together, eventually within a couple of months of meeting getting our kids together in a park one Sunday afternoon. The meeting of families went reasonably well and my kids certainly took to her. Bonds were formed and strengthened and the relationship flourished.

To trust and be trusted
I do not intend to account for every episode in this relationship from beginning to end but at this point I would like to draw out a couple of key lessons that I believe I could have and certainly should have learned during the relationship. I won't identify them as Golden Rules since at this point my kids and my shared-parenting were not even a factor in these lessons.

I stated above when talking about lessons learned in dating, the importance of knowing what you want and of being true to yourself and committed to achieving those things. One of the main lessons that I took from this relationship and which became a headline statement in my online dating profile subsequently was that I needed to be with someone *who I could trust, and who I would be trusted by*. In short, these sentiments stemmed from the fact that throughout the relationship there were repeated instances of me being unjustly accused of being unfaithful to her, of not being trustworthy and of trying to deceive or mis-lead her. These episodes are mentioned out of the blue and out of context deliberately since the circumstances that lead to some of these groundless accusations are frankly ridiculous no matter how I try and capture and relay the circumstances that led to them, to you now. In the context of shared-parenting and indicative of the substance behind many of the accusations was that she simply could not cope with the ongoing communication, dialogue and co-operation that I had with my ex. This may have been due to experiences in her past, or merely because it didn't echo with her own experience with her ex and the father of her daughter. Either way, it was largely irrelevant since it placed a real pressure on what was otherwise at many points a happy and fulfilling relationship.

Experience showed me very many times in the course of my relationship with her, that there are few things more soul-destroying in a relationship, than to have to spend your life feeling like you are constantly under-suspicion regarding what you are doing, who you are doing it with and why you are doing it, when all you are trying to do is live your life according to your own moral-code.

I can understand that many reading this book who have either been cheated-on, or who have been unfaithful in relationships will understand and appreciate the fundamental importance of being able to trust and be trusted to longevity in relationships. I can say that in my case, *none* of the accusations were just or warranted. By the end of our relationship I truly felt like I was living in a constant state of scrutiny and mistrust.

The ex and the new partner

I don't suppose that many people will encounter the ex-partner or ex-wife/husband of their new partner and immediately feel warmly towards them. First and foremost, it is likely that prior to meeting them, you will have heard at least an abridged or sanitized version of the reasons why your relationship failed. Whether the issues that caused the separation are a catalogue of minor-wrongs that just pointed to incompatibility, or whether there were more serious factors at play such as infidelity or even abuse, you are unlikely to be drawn to the person who in some way caused hurt to the person you are contemplating spending the rest of your life with.

I wouldn't dare to expect that anyone who ever met my ex to feel any differently just because I share the parenting of our children. Fundamentally she and I had our issues which prevented our marriage from enduring; I contributed to this failing but so did she and whilst there will always be sides of the story that I don't wish to share with others, there are things that I have discussed with subsequent partners regarding the failing of my marriage, just as I'm realistic that she will have done the same.

What I think is somewhat different in my circumstance is that it should be apparent to anyone who has become involved with me is that whilst the differences that caused me to part from my ex are acknowledged by us both, we have sought to put aside our differences to allow us to focus on the parenting of the kids we had together in the best way that we possibly can. As you will hopefully appreciate from what you have read in this book, this arrangement demands a greater level of contact between me and my ex than others may feel comfortable with. The fundamental basis of this is in effectively handling all matters relating to the parenting of our kids; that is where it begins and ends.

I am not so blinkered as to think that some people wouldn't still have a problem with the above set up due to it not being particularly traditional, but I also recognise that this is likely to be prompted by the fact that the set-up is different to their own. What I always hoped would be the case for any future partner that I have, would be that whilst I wouldn't expect them to get on with, or even like my ex necessarily (although I can see nothing about her that makes her inherently unlikeable and if I can get on with her, I don't see why others cannot) I *would* expect them to at least allow my relationship to continue unhindered for the benefit of my kids. When I say allow, I am not suggesting that I am so weak-willed as to feel that I need permission for how I live aspects of my life but I am talking about my deserving of the space to get on with it without criticism or comment.

My ex and I have always had an understanding that as and when we entered into new relationships and once the kids were familiar with these people, at some point thereafter we would make it possible for them to meet each other should there be a suitable opportunity. Speaking for myself, I wouldn't ever put myself in a position of wanting to somehow 'audition' the new partner of my ex or to even expect to be asked what I thought of them (in fact, I'd rather not be asked frankly, as it is really none of my business). However, I do appreciate having the opportunity to at least meet even if only in passing the person who my kids now know and may be spending at least a portion of their time around. I am sure the same is true of my ex.

Failure to protect the shared-parenting arrangement
When difficulties were apparent in the lack of acceptance of my shared-parenting arrangement, and the comfort that was felt (or rather that was lacking) regarding my relationship with my ex the consequences still didn't need to be inevitable in terms of affecting it. The sad truth though is that I failed to protect the sanctity of the shared-parenting arrangement and did at the time what I thought was the best I could to accommodate my new partner's feelings and protect her from the source of misguided insecurity.

In attempting to manage her insecurity I allowed communication with the mother of my children to be cut, monitored and curtailed. I reduced the amicability of the overall setup by reducing the informal nature of our communication and the facility for my ex to contact the kids when they were with me and also reduced my interaction with my ex and the kids when they were with her. In essence, I tried to limit the contact and make the whole thing much more formal and as a result, inherently more stilted as a means of trying to assuage irrational jealousy and insecurity on the part of my new partner.

This of course backfired massively and the net effects were that I harmed the relationship with my ex, I was able to see the kids less than I wanted and the very fabric of my shared-parenting arrangement was under threat. And the worst thing about all of this was that *I had let this happen.* Looking back on this I don't apportion blame to anyone but myself for allowing this to happen. I had effectively sold-out the most important thing in my life, my kids in allowing the shared-parenting arrangement that was in place to best serve their needs to be impacted upon and threatened by the new relationship in my life and it has taken a long while for me to come back from this.

Obviously, this would not have come about without the causes and difficulties originating from the new relationship which were brought along by my new partner, but the fact remains that I let it happen. In spite of me trying to convey that my focus was on being able to support my shared-parenting of the kids through my relationship with my ex-wife as I had done for years, there was clearly unfounded suspicion that in some way I still harboured feelings for and a desire to get back with her. My new partner presumably thought that the same existed in reverse between my ex-wife and me. In reality this couldn't be further from the truth, but through my colluding with these accusations instead of standing firm, I had effectively entered into the game and from this point on the relationship really was doomed.

> *Golden Rule #13* – It is imperative that you protect and preserve the sanctity and structure of your shared-parenting arrangement as you would protect your kids themselves. Do not allow yourself to be swayed by others be they friends, family, new partners or acquaintances in terms of being forced to modify any aspect unless it is specifically for the benefit of the children. In this case, such changes should be discussed and agreed with the person whom you share the parenting with.

The above Golden Rule cannot be emphasized enough. Whilst I have introduced it in the context of my experience in a new relationship, it is equally applicable to influences that could arise from any other person in your life. This could be anyone who may feel that it is their business to exert influence on you to change your approach to shared-parenting for any reason other than one which might benefit the children. Examples of this could come up for a variety of reasons and of course I am not suggesting that you should be so blinkered as to ignore anything that anyone says about your life and the choices you have made. I have emphasized in the chapter on detractors and naysayers above that shared-parenting can attract a variety of comments and feedback, both positive and negative. I think it is a foolish person who is oblivious to everything that everyone else says. However, it is essential that you are guarded against being coerced into changing your shared-parenting arrangement for *any* reason and should anyone suggest a change (either directly to the arrangement or to some other aspect of your life that could impact upon it) then you must consider this in terms of what is motivating them and whether it is a change that will serve any benefit to your children. I guess this is another way of drawing you back to consider Golden Rule #1!

Being true to yourself

One of the most contentious points that was discussed time and again in this relationship was the question over whether or not there existed the prospect or mutual desire to have children together. You may recall that my viewpoint on whether I wanted to have more kids has always been based firmly in the position that I was convinced that I didn't really want to have more. There had been the slight ambiguity in my online dating profile whereby I had stated that if I met 'the one' then this might change, and I stand by the intention behind that statement at the time, since we cannot know everything about ourselves at every point in life. That said, I am now 100% convinced that I never want to have more kids of my own.

The point I was trying to convey at the time was that although I knew how I felt in my heart and mind, it was not possible to say at that point in my early thirties that this couldn't change. However, I was clear to articulate that it was more the case that I wasn't open to be persuaded but more that it was a change in feeling that might come about from within myself.

The stumbling block in my mind that would always have haunted me even if I felt convinced that I did want kids in a new relationship was that I didn't *ever* want to be in a position again where I brought about further kids into this world and didn't feel 100% assured that I would be in a stable and secure relationship with their other parent for the rest of my days. The fact of the matter is that it *is* complex to run a shared-parenting arrangement and to balance all other aspects of life alongside it (or at least sufficiently so that I haven't particularly struggled to fill a book on the subject!) I cannot conceive of the challenge that would be associated with running two such arrangements with two sets of kids to different mothers. I would be extremely interested in talking to anyone who does so to understand how this works!

It was with this consideration in the back of my mind that I entered into such discussions and gave airing to the view that having kids together may at some point be a prospect if I felt that we were in a loving, trusting and secure relationship that would form the stable back-drop for the raising of these kids for the rest of our lives together. My second great failing in this relationship was that I ever voiced the opinion that there was any ambiguity in my mind about this possibility, but should instead just have let things evolve, and to allow life to take its course which would no doubt have led to the same conclusion, that of the failing of that relationship.

The key stumbling block that affected the longevity of the relationship and the stability that I felt was really down to my being treated with suspicion and mistrust on a routine basis for no logical or genuine reason. Many other aspects of my life suffered as a result of this, and again solely because I let them change and didn't protect my own interests adequately. I seldom socialised with friends since there was always the risk that it might be suspected that I were up to no good whilst out and about. I felt less able to speak regularly to my parents since I was fearful that as the people who knew me best, they would sense something was not right. The key issue in taking these courses of action is that by doing what I did, I was entering into her game and adding fuel to the fire rather than standing by my own actions and decisions and conducting myself as someone who had nothing to hide or defend.

What I have learned conclusively as a part of this relationship, and many others that I have had are a few key things.

1) It is not possible to fix other people's issues. We *all* have issues, baggage, preconceptions, prejudices, ingrained reactions to things and instincts that are based on past experiences. In my view it is the responsibility of the individual to know themselves, to do what they can to process these things and to be honest with themselves and with others about who they are, what they are about and what they need. In the words of my sister, we each need to "sort our own shit out before we involve ourselves in someone else's". As much as you may want to help someone to deal with their issues, both for their benefit and for your own it is simply not possible to do that since the drive and desire to do so has to come within the individual.

2) A fair, equitable and equal relationship will not feature one or both partners having to make repeated concessions or compromises in order to keep the other person happy beyond what you would reasonably do for the maintenance of harmony and fairness. It *is* fair to each take a turn at the washing-up, to contribute equally to looking after the kids, to go and see a movie that appeals to your partner that you might not fancy, just because they want you to. It *isn't* fair to expect your partner to cease all contact with friends of the other just because it makes you feel uncomfortable and suspicious of their motives. A happy and functional relationship cannot be based upon such bending out of shape by one party to accommodate the other.

3) It is *fundamentally* important for the individual to be consistent and true to themselves, and to not waver on things that are of primary importance to the other person, if they do not have a committed intention on following through on this, or are not able to commit to this without caveats. I maintain that my views on whether or not I would ever have further kids in a relationship have always been consistent since I parted from the mother of my kids; any

prospect of having a child together was contingent on my feeling completely secure in a new relationship, on me being as certain as I could ever be that the relationship would endure and that we would never part. I don't think that this was unreasonable of me. What I could have done differently though would have been to explicitly state this as my view on the matter and to never waver on the subject.

Golden Rule #14 – As you enter into new relationships, and indeed as you contemplate any major life changes, ensure that you are being 100% true to yourself and ensuring that you don't waver on the things that are essential to you in living the life you want. Failing to do this will impact upon your happiness as a person, and on your ability to be the parent that you want to be to your kids.

The lengths we go to

One of the turning points in the relationship came at the point at which she and her child moved into my home. This felt at the time like a natural progression for the relationship and was also an attempt on my part to allay some of her insecurity over my belief in and commitment to our relationship.

Aside from the wider potential impacts and the further reaching effects that this decision would prove to have on my life, it also represented the crossing of a line in regard to my kids and the impact that this relationship would have on my shared-parenting arrangement. The obvious effects of this change upon my kids (notwithstanding whether things worked out or not) were going to be:

- That our house would cease to be mine and the kids home, but would be home to all of us. Symbolically this represented a huge shift for my kids in terms of sharing their space.
- That whilst they would continue to live with me (us) for one week in two, due to the less structured arrangement that she had with the father of her child, there would be extensive periods of time when my kids would not be with me but they would know that her child was at their home. For them, this was a potential threat, I am sure, to their perception of their place in my life, and also in terms of the child having the run of the house and the ability to mess with their possessions when they weren't there.
- That fundamentally there would be an unprecedented need to share everything in their world (at my house) with two other people.

What amazed me at the time was that whilst I could foresee that these things would be a big deal to the kids, they outwardly seemed to take all this in their stride and were actually really supportive and encouraging about the forthcoming change. It is one of the many things that I love about my kids that they are so very adaptable and supportive of anything that they feel will make me happy. I genuinely hope that this has never shrouded their true feelings on things and that they were never just trying to tell me what they thought I wanted to hear (even though I suspect this might have at times been the case). Having planned the process of moving her and her child into the house that was as sensitive to everyone's needs as it could be, we undertook to make this a reality.

I do not intend to account for all the time that passed when we subsequently became engaged (another step I misguidedly took to try and reassure her of my commitment) and started to live together. What was more or less immediately apparent was that it did not provide the fix to the problems that I had hoped it would either in making her feel more secure, or in allowing me to believe the relationship would truly endure. The severe impacts of having to manage the aftermath of these episodes in the much more pressurised environment where we were all in a single home and there wasn't the separate home to retreat to made it all the more difficult to recover from such episodes. There were certainly good times that we all shared as an amalgamated family unit but looking back on it I would say that little more than 3 months after they moved in, we had passed a point whereby the final split that culminated in them moving out a few months later had become an inevitability.

The blended family

Whilst the relationship ultimately failed, we spent a few months living together with a 'blended' family unit and in this period I learned a number of things that I hope may be useful to anyone in a shared-parenting arrangement looking to move in with a new partner (or a new partner and their children). Should I ever be in the position to contemplate this again, I will certainly be keeping these factors in mind.

Lesson 1 – Everyone needs to adopt the mind-set of it being 'our home' rather than being the preserve of those whose home it was. This is easier to say than to enact, however it is essential that steps are taken so that all people feel that the home is theirs equally. For us, this involved a strategy of reallocating space in the house so that each of the kids still had their own bedroom so that they had space to call their own and to feel association with. This is somewhat different though to making everything in the house immediately be communal property. This was particularly the case in relation to her child, since she was at the house a lot of the time when my kids were not, and the child needed to be clear that it wasn't their realm to just use the rooms and possessions of my kids as they pleased when my kids weren't there. I am keen to emphasize to my kids the importance of sharing, but my rationale is that I want their home with me to feel the same as it would if they were with me full-time and if they were with me full time I wouldn't expect them to accept that another child had free-run of their space or their possessions any more than this would apply in reverse.

Lesson 2 – If you are going to the lengths of moving, this must be undertaken 'wholesale'. It is entirely feasible that your new partner may not live in the same town as you, and their kids may be at different schools. We quickly found that it was logistically challenging for her child to continue attending a different school that was now around half an hour away, and so took the decision that they would move to the school local to my home. Whilst this was not a decision taken lightly, it made logistical sense and although another complicating event at the time and was one of the positives that lasted following the breakdown of the relationship. My suggestion therefore is that if you are seriously committed to establishing a blended family, you should really consider establishing it on the basis that the kids are all educated locally and that some move schools, effectively ensuring that all of you are fully committed and entrenched in your new life together. This of course makes the move all the more serious and impactful but I would assert that this is not a decision to take lightly at all and so perhaps any additional considerations such as the kids having to change schools will ensure that you have explored all angles and associated aspects of the change.

Lesson 3 – Is it essential to taking things in the direction you want them to? I am trying to disentangle the lessons associated with the establishment of a blended family from the personal lessons I have taken from this relationship and others. A long-term future in a committed relationship can be something that can be demonstrated and managed in a variety of ways and doesn't necessarily demand that major steps need to be taken within the immediate timeframe (moving in, getting engaged, even marrying). Ensure that things happen at a pace that works for everyone (keeping Golden Rule #1 at the fore, of course).

Lesson 4 – There needs to be a redistribution of roles in the family. As I mentioned earlier in the book, I feel it is essential that the various diverse roles that need to be fulfilled to make a relationship work and it is essential to understand and agree who does what in a relationship so that everyone has clarity and no-one is taken for granted. The specific nature of these roles and how you define and allocate them will be shaped by the circumstances of you and your partner and it could well depend on whether you both work, whether one or other of you has other responsibilities or commitments and other factors that will dictate how things are managed. Such considerations need to be given adequate thought and then allocated so that each of you feels that things are fair and equitable. In this instance, this may well encompass discussions regarding joint-finances, parental responsibility, child-care arrangements and so-on, and whilst protecting your shared-parenting arrangement you may well both be required to make significant changes to the way in which you manage your lives generally.

Lesson 5 – You may need to adapt the 'rules of the house'. This aligns with adapting to the 'our home' mind-set and is essential if all the kids are going to feel like it is all their homes. There would undoubtedly been two sets of rules at each of the two houses prior to you all moving in together (four sets if you count the ex-partners) and so it is important that a new baseline of behaviour is established so that all the kids know where they stand. These rules will be dictated to an extent by what age the kids are, but in our home they were things such as whether the kids were allowed food and drink on the sofa, whether they had to take their shoes off inside the house and fairly low-level functional things. For older kids this may focus on expectations around when homework must be done, bed-times, curfews, whether you all sit down for meals together or not and other such considerations. There is no single way or set of rules that will work for everyone but the key thing is that there should be one set of rules for all the kids in the house to avoid a 'them and us' scenario.

Lesson 6 – All kids must be dealt with fairly and equitably by both adults and each adult must be given equal respect by the kids. This is undoubtedly one of the hardest things to introduce and yet probably the single most important factor to success. It is a great challenge for each adult to treat all the kids equally and based on my experience the tendency is to over-compensate in both directions; to be somewhat more positive towards your partner's child in order to bond with them and slightly harder on your own kids in order to demonstrate to your partner that you are not showing them unreasonable favour. The challenge is instead to be fair towards all, and ensure that praise and punishment are meted out equally by both adults to all kids. Only by doing this consistently and for the long term will the kids gain the faith that this is how things now work in the new blended-household.

The end of the road

I have stated at many points in this chapter that it is not my intention to have written a detailed account of every aspect of this relationship, but more that I wanted to draw out the aspects that are relevant to shared-parenting. Whilst I have provided a fair bit of contextual information, my intention in doing so is to add substance to the lessons that I believe can be taken from the experience in the hope that these may be transferrable to others.

There was only one possible conclusion for this relationship and whilst it took longer to come about than it should, ultimately we reached the end. It was an end that also incorporated a reasonable amount of upset, upheaval and discord for all involved. This is one of my greatest regrets about the whole relationship; my split from my ex-wife many years before had a great deal more at stake in that we were married, we had mutual assets (and debts) to distribute and most importantly we had to determine how we would still give our kids the best life we could. With this added burden, I believe that we still managed to do this with care and consideration, respect and dignity in a way that minimized the impact on the kids. In stark contrast this later split was messy, undignified and unpleasant for all involved; that I had brought about this relationship voluntarily and involved my kids in it knowingly made me feel all the worse for its effect on them (and also for the impact it no doubt had on her child).

The lasting effects of this relationship have been significant for me. Many of the lessons that I had learned from my experience of dating, as summarised in a previous chapter, crystallised for me following this relationship and as such in the aftermath I feel I have a much greater understanding of the importance of many of these lessons; most of all the need to be true to who you are and what you want, and of not committing yourself to things too quickly.

One of the most important lessons I learned though, was in relation to my own personal views on guilt, and how I have handled guilt in the past. I felt enormous guilt at the parting of this relationship and felt a real need to develop and practice coping mechanisms to deal with it. I would like to share these with you now.

Chapter 11 – Dealing with the guilt

At this point, as we near the end of my 'guide' to shared-parenting (guide is a grandiose term I think, but I would hope that it has the capacity to at least provide some pointers in the right general direction, if not a full-scale, 3 dimensional map of how to get there), I want to include a chapter on guilt and coping with guilt.

I feel this is appropriate since I know from my own personal experience that learning about guilt, how to deal with it effectively and how to manage its influence in my day-to-day life has been a key part of allowing me to move forwards in life and to be the best person and father that I could be. I'm still no expert at it but I feel that I have learned a lot and I would like to be able to impart some of that knowledge and experience to you in the hope that it helps you too. I emphasize that this is based on my own analysis of the emotion, my interpretation of the impacts of it and my views on how to manage it. It is not based on proven psychological analysis or research but I hope that it may be applicable or of interest at least to others.

Guilt is an extremely corrosive, negative and wearing emotion that can hinder each and every aspect of our lives if we allow it to. It has the power to make us question the worth and the validity of what we are doing, whilst undermining our belief in ourselves and our fundamental trust in our own ability to do the right thing. It can erode away at you until you feel unable to confidently undertake the most simple of tasks with any enthusiasm or conviction and can destroy your self-confidence if you are not mindful of it and watchful for it taking its effect on you. As is normally the case with anything that you don't want or don't need, there is guilt to be taken at every turn if you leave yourself open to it.

In the weeks and months immediately following my split from Jo the main emotion that I felt aside from general upset was that of guilt. At the outset of us meeting and with the subsequent pregnancy that quickly ensued I felt like I was ready, willing and able to take on the world and do whatever was necessary to prove that I could do the thing that all around me were telling me was the impossible (and which inside I was telling myself if I had let myself admit it); to make a successful go of life as a young guy at the outset of his career and fatherhood, simultaneously trying to make the best job possible of both of these roles.

A little over 5 event-filled years later, whilst I could point to many significant achievements and some extremely happy times, fundamentally I had failed to achieve what I had set out to do and this troubled me greatly. I felt guilty for having let Jo down in not being able to do what was necessary to make our marriage work (even though I knew that the failing wasn't solely my own, but a combination of factors that meant neither of us was really to blame, just that it wasn't ever going to be 'right'). I felt guilty for having failed in my parents' eyes (even though I knew that they weren't viewing it as such and were just concerned for everyone's happiness). Most of all I felt guilty for failing my kids, for not being able to give them the stable and happy family life that I had been lucky enough to rely on throughout my life and for being partially responsible for giving rise to a situation that I knew was going to take a significant toll on their happiness and sense of stability as things unravelled.

After the initial period of what can best be described as mourning for the passing of my relationship I quickly recognised that things needed to be done to allow me to move on with the business of life and of making a fresh start. To do this successfully was going to require me to take control of my emotions and to allow myself to function in the numerous roles that were now mine to deliver. I needed to adapt to the task at hand and whilst I don't necessarily feel it is possible to control guilt, in common with many emotions it is possible to condition the way in which you react to it.

How guilt arises

Put simply, I believe that guilt arises when our sub-conscious mind analyses (or more likely, repeatedly-analyses) situations within which we feel bad the minute our involvement with them has occurred, and ensures that this negativity is linked-in to our actions and the things we have said and done. Guilt is our mind's way of punishing ourselves, of ensuring we fixate on the negatives of an event rather than its opposite; pride, where we capture the positives associated with a happening or event and feel good about it. The fact is that bad things happen all the time but we can learn from them and improve, striving to ensure that they don't happen again or we can become crippled by negativity that prevents us from managing on a day to day basis.

I will illustrate my thinking with an example; my kids may be having a disagreement over something or other, usually at a time when I am coming to the end of a stressful and hectic day. I may lose my temper and shout at the one of them who I believe to be the instigator of the argument. Almost the second that I have shouted (whilst me shouting may or may not serve any useful purpose in resolving the issue at hand) I immediately feel that familiar, nagging sense of being ill-at-ease, of feeling like what I have done is wrong. In my mind I will question myself:

- Did I shout at the right child?
- Was shouting really appropriate given the magnitude of their argument?
- Was my response proportionate to the event?

- Did my response make any difference?
- Was all I really achieved to scare one or other of the kids?
- Will my shouting on this occasion serve any useful purpose to me in that the next time they have a similar argument I will remember that all I really did last time was to make myself feel bad?
- Will it have any consequence to the kids the next time they are bickering, will they stop themselves and think that they should probably stop arguing?

The answers to those questions could be numerous and varied depending on how I am feeling at the time and in most cases are irrelevant to either the outcome of the situation in hand, and to future events as well. Put simply the process serves only one real purpose and that is to add that little marker in my subconscious of yet another event that has happened for which I feel bad. My guilt burden has thus increased a little as a result.

The above example, whilst a little convoluted is intended to demonstrate my theory of the process by which we build up a burden of guilt for ourselves each and every day, via events ranging from the most trivial of interactions through to major happenings in our lives.

I don't think that the average, rational, decent person can stop themselves from feeling guilt but what is most important is the way in which we respond to the guilty feelings, to the internal questioning and to the feeling that this prompts which in turn determines the impact this has on our life. I speculate that the average psychopath or serial killer feels very little in the way of guilt; they don't question what they do, don't feel remorse for what they have done, and move through life pretty much unconcerned by things that happen as a result of their actions. As an aside, I've also encountered a number of people who seem to pass through life with this philosophy too, as I'm sure you have; I wonder if they actually possess other psychopathic tendencies? Anyway, I digress.

I believe that to strive for the 'psychopathic' position in regard to guilt would mean that we had lost a certain amount of our inherent humanity, and certainly that we had closed our minds to any desire to learn from our mistakes and generally to grow to be a better person. I feel there is a middle ground for handling feelings of guilt and one such way is that which I have found allows me to get on with life just a little bit more effectively.

The events that prompt guilt cannot be avoided and should not be ignored. We feel guilt since as generally good and decent human beings we know when we have done something that is at odds with our personal moral code or how we wish to be as people and in life. It is about what we do with those feelings and how we allow ourselves to absorb the lessons and move forward that determines the effect these feelings have on us. It seems to me that the two alternatives are to process the lesson as positively as possible and move forward, or to allow the burden of guilt to weigh us down and for it to even start a downward spiral of effects. Naturally my preference is to try and achieve the former!

Consider the example above of shouting at the kids. If I contemplate the questions that came up in my mind, then the most negative answers that I could provide would be as follows:

- Did I shout at the right child? *Probably not, or maybe it was both of their faults*
- Was shouting really appropriate given the magnitude of their argument? *No, they are just being kids, and kids fight over trivial things.*

- Was my response proportionate to the event? *No, and I treated them as though they had done far worse than they were doing.*
- Did my response make any difference? *No, they were just shocked and hurt by my reaction*
- Was all I really achieved to scare one or other of the kids? Will my shouting on this occasion serve any useful purpose to me in that the next time they have a similar argument I will remember that all I really did last time was to make myself feel bad? *No, they will inevitably fight again, and I will no doubt shout again as I always do*
- Will it have any consequence to the kids the next time they are bickering, will they stop themselves and think that they should probably stop arguing? *No, they will no doubt have forgotten about it and argue again over equally trivial things.*

This would lead me to the broad conclusion that my actions in shouting had been disproportionate, misguided and ineffective in dealing with the issue at hand. I have probably hurt the kids' feelings as well.

If I answer the questions with the most positive answers possible, the conclusion still isn't going to be much different since whilst I may mentally let myself off the harm or hurt that I may have done by losing my temper and shouting, it is unlikely that the net effect will be any different in terms of their future behaviour. In either case I doubt that there would be any lasting effects from my shouting, either on the kids developing an inherent mistrust or fear of me or in terms of having some preventative effect on them bickering in future. The only difference is that with the negative thought process around the guilt questions that my mind throws up, if I don't take the negative thought process into check, I risk going to the darker place where the guilt starts to weigh me down. I make myself susceptible to the negative thought process that goes like this:

- I always shout at the kids for no reason, therefore:
- I have no patience or tolerance for kids just being kids, therefore:
- I am a terrible father

And so it continues.

Breaking the cycle

The example above is given to illustrate the process rather than to prompt a debate on the rights and wrongs of shouting at kids. What I hope it illustrates is that the events that can prompt guilt are numerous and various in the scale of the questions they may prompt in our subconscious, the guilt burden it may saddle us with (if we let it) and the downward spiral that it may take us on if we don't harness the thoughts and feelings and recognise them for what they are; unhelpful questions that we pose to ourselves that aren't going to affect either the outcomes of the event that has already happened, or the lasting effects of it.

As with most problems and difficulties that we are presented with in life, the first step to handling it is acknowledgement or understanding of the issue at hand. It is my contention therefore that the better way of dealing with the feelings above is first and foremost to recognise them as they come up, and know them for what they are. In this example, I'm not saying that it is immediately okay to excuse oneself for shouting at the kids or let events pass unquestioned just because you immediately recognise the feelings as guilt-based, or as potentially leading to feelings of guilt. The key thing is to see it as it is; in this example he kids were acting up and arguing over something, presumably to such a degree that it caused enough anger to shout. This may not necessarily have warranted shouting, but was shouting the worst thing you could have done? No, you could have dragged them apart and sent them to their rooms (potentially much more disproportionate to what was likely to be nothing more than childish bickering). Or you could have left them to it which could have both let it escalate until blows were exchanged, or alternatively/simultaneously sent them the subconscious message that it is acceptable to fight and argue over trivial things. Indeed, shouting might have been excessive but under the circumstance it was certainly not the worst thing, and the fact that you care enough to want to try and shape their behaviour makes you a better parent than those who allow their kids' behaviour to remain unchecked, bordering on the feral! The reasonable conclusion at the end of this thought process is certainly not one of "I am a terrible father" but I believe it also leaves enough room for you to remain mindful of the fact that it didn't feel good to shout and you would like not to shout again under the same circumstances. Fundamentally you are not beating yourself up for having done so, a fact that you cannot go back in time and change anyway.

In my view the key to handling guilt effectively is, at a basic level affording yourself the mental space, capacity and freedom to learn lessons without unduly shackling yourself with an enormous and weighty guilt burden that prevents you from moving forwards. It takes time to adopt this mentality and there are a number of techniques that I suggest you can adopt, and mental pointers that you can give yourself to assist in making this your reaction:

- **Avoid the 'what-if' questions** – In analysing your past actions and decisions, the asking of 'what-if' questions is harmful since it focusses your mind on how virtually any theoretical set of actions or circumstances would have brought about a better conclusion than the actions you took. This is pointless and only serves to make you feel worse.

- **Have a clear and realistic purpose about all that you do** – It should be possible for all of your actions to be brought back to a simple basic purpose. In the context of the example above my purpose is to raise two well-adjusted kids who are self-aware and who know how to behave and recognise good and bad behaviour in themselves and in others. If you can articulate the basic purpose of your actions (to yourself first and foremost), you then have a useful framework against which to assess your actions and pragmatically consider what is causing you to feel guilt. For example, if your broad purpose is to eat healthily to improve your overall physical health and lose weight, and you have just eaten a box of donuts, then your reaction may be of guilt for taking yourself off course. However, you can consider this a minor bump in the road and get back on track which will make you feel better since this will align with your overall purpose. Alternatively you can then excuse yourself to have a milkshake as well, as you already feel miserable (knowing that this will make you feel even more miserable deep down since it isn't aligned with your overall purpose). In either case you are making a conscious decision against some point of reference rather than letting it set you off on a negative spiral of thoughts that would inevitably lead off on a tangent and increase your guilt burden.
- **Be realistic with yourself about what is important in the wider scheme of things** – There is nothing wrong with aiming at and aspiring for the best, but what is problematic is *expecting* the best. Feelings of guilt are often prompted or at least exacerbated by placing unrealistic expectations on ourselves or on those around us. I aspire for the best for my kids in life generally and my aim is to raise them to be polite and responsible individuals. I find myself feeling disappointment when I *expect* the best from them and it does not materialise and then I feel guilty for feeling

disappointed in them, and so the downward spiral begins. What is far more healthy and helpful to ourselves and to others is to be realistic about what is important to us, and why. Recognising what is important allows a more measured effort to be devoted to the things that really matter, and more proportionate reactions when things don't go as we would like them to.

The tips above are deliberately simple and few, since it is easiest in life to make small changes and tweaks. I genuinely believe that incorporating some or all of these will be of assistance in turning around your reactions to incidents that give rise to guilt.

As I have emphasized throughout this chapter, I do not pretend to have studied all aspects of guilt nor am I sufficiently qualified to position myself as an expert on any such matters. What I am though is someone who at periods in their life has given themselves cause to feel guilty for the lasting effects of their actions. I know the damaging effect that this has had on my ability at times to deal with the challenges that life has presented me in the best way I could.

Through a growing self-awareness and the development of a number of coping mechanisms that I have outlined above, I feel I have heightened my own ability to handle such feelings. Whilst I don't pretend to have a handle on all aspects of the management of guilt, I know that these methods work for me. I hope that they may work for you since I have learned that in fulfilling the challenging role of single parent whether in a shared-parenting arrangement or not, there is enormous scope for guilt to arise. It is in what you do with this guilt that determines what its lasting effects will be, either as a source of negativity in your life or as a prompt for positive reflection or change.

Chapter 12 – Looking to the future

I hope that somewhere buried in the anecdotes, stories, Golden Rules and Lessons above you will have found at least something of use or interest to you. Maybe you just found it reassuring that you are not the only person to have gone through an experience that you and I have shared. Perhaps it has offered you a few pointers that you will be able to apply to your situation as a parent, or maybe it has simply reaffirmed what you were already doing. Maybe you found it a tedious read from beginning to end, and have only soldiered-on as you had nothing better to do. I hope it's not the latter.

My motivations when I set out to write this book were numerous. First, I wanted to test out that old cliché that 'everyone has a book in them'; I love a challenge! Secondly, whilst I would accept that I'm not the most interesting guy on the planet and my experiences are not akin to having scaled Everest without oxygen or having crossed the Serengeti on a micro-scooter, I do feel that the events that I have described within this book have been some kind of adventure. It has thrust upon me numerous challenges, difficulties, opportunities and rewards along the way. I am someone who can't help but think about things endlessly, and I think that the conclusions and lessons that I've drawn are my best possible explanation as to how and why things work and why, to some degree I have emerged from the adventure (up until now), unscathed.

This is certainly not to say that I believe I have all the answers or that I am kidding myself that I have completed the adventure. There have been numerous things that have no doubt played an important part in things working out as they have. I am blessed with two amazing kids whose resilience, good nature and adaptability is dwarfed only by their loving nature. That said I would like to think that it is hard to draw the line between cause and effect, as I genuinely believe that part of who they are has been shaped by the shared-parenting arrangement that their mother and I have used to raise them in the last 10 or so years. When they are adults, should they choose that path, I will of course wish for them a family life that follows convention and that they never have to suffer the inevitable pain or complications in life that accompany a split. However, it gives me comfort that they already know there is an alternative to the standard/traditional raising of a family by two parents, and that has been demonstrated to them in their own upbringing; an upbringing that I genuinely believe has been positive in its own right rather than merely the best possible substitute under negative circumstances.

I am reluctant for you to think that I am sat here congratulating myself on a job well done and thinking that I'm through the worst; my eldest daughter just reached the age of 16, and another 4 years parenting two teenage daughters stretch out before me. If the last few years haven't been testing enough, I'm sure the next few certainly will be. What I am confident of though is that between us, their mother and I will continue to apply Golden Rule #1 and ensure that we make the best joint parenting decisions that we can for the benefit of our kids. Furthermore, until they are self-sufficient adults their Mum and I will maintain the communication and collaborative approach to ensure that we present a united front in the guidance that we give them. Indeed, this will continue for the rest of their lives.

The thing that has always been present in my mind since I first learned that I was to be a parent was that this role, the responsibilities that it carries and the expectations that it brings with it, are for life. I will always be a father to my daughters. This is of course the case for all parents regardless of their background or philosophies, whether they choose to be involved in the raising of their kids or not. I know that for me it is the most important role that I will ever fill and I am extremely grateful that the circumstances of my life have allowed me to play the role that I do in my kids' lives. Factors such as an acrimonious ex-wife, a long-term illness or other factors that affected my ability to be a father in a shared-parenting arrangement would of course have led to a different outcome for my kids and me, and to be honest still could. What I like to think would be true for me, and why I feel that much of the content of this book is applicable to others whose circumstance as parents may be different to mine, is that the core principles can be extended to all parents. This is true whether you are a single-father or single-mother, whether your child's other parent is present in their lives or not, whether you get as much contact with your kids as you would like, or whether you are forced to go down legal channels to get access to your kids.

Regardless which of the circumstances above apply to you, you will hopefully agree with and benefit from adopting the ethos that is suggested in the majority of Golden Rules which I have summarised below:

Golden Rule #1 – Each and every action, decision and guiding principle must be based around the needs of the kids and what is best for them.

Golden Rule #2 – The fundamental basis of the shared-parenting arrangement must be structured, repeatable, and enduring in its design to allow it to benefit the children (see Golden Rule #1) and to meet the needs of the parents

Golden Rule #3 – In combination with rigidity and structure, a shared-parenting arrangement must be able to flex as the needs of the child and the circumstances surrounding the arrangement (either short or long term) change.

Golden Rule #4 – Once Golden Rule #1 has been satisfied, it is okay for the shared-parenting arrangement to be designed for the mutual and individual benefit of the parents. Ensure though that it is equally beneficial otherwise resentments and negativity will creep in.

Golden Rule #5 – In agreeing the terms of a shared-parenting arrangement, there must be a consideration of the overall sustainability of the arrangement, and the effects it will have on the quality of life of the kids and the parents. If the terms of the arrangement require excessive compromise, expenditure, travel, or efforts to be made on a long-term basis then it is likely that the arrangement will at some point cease to work for everyone and may ultimately fail.

Golden Rule #6 –The financial terms of a shared-parenting arrangement should always be negotiated, reviewed, managed and implemented separately from any other financial arrangements associated with the dissolution of the relationship. Treat any on-going payments that are not split equally between the parents as being focussed on the kids and maintain this distinction. Review the arrangement regularly and strive for an equitable 50/50 split.

Golden Rule #7 –Once you have agreed to move forwards with the shared-parenting arrangement, establish it and immediately start living it (or do so as soon as it is realistically viable to). Apply the same approach to other key decisions, changes and in dealing with events that will doubtlessly occur and need to be managed throughout the arrangement. The time for action is always NOW.

Golden Rule #8 – It is advisable to think about a structured way of doing things, to help adapt to and maintain the shared-parenting arrangement, in as much or as little detail as you feel appropriate to yours and your kids' needs. Expect though that your structures and rules may be different from those of your ex, and don't feel pressured to adapt to their way of working. The key thing is that your overall goals, beliefs, aspirations and priorities for your kids are aligned which will ensure that your kids have a consistent parenting experience across both homes.

Golden Rule #9 – Whilst both parents are unlikely to agree on all matters that require a united-front of parenting, the key thing is to agree on the over-arching principles that shape your shared-parenting arrangement. Within this, matters such as expectations for the kids' behaviour, your aspirations and goals for them, the freedoms and disciplines you want them to grow-up with and the priorities for their upbringing should be understood and agreed upon by you both.

Golden Rule #10 – Where possible, agree on an approach to presenting a united front that ensures a level of trust and autonomy is given by Mum and Dad to each other to deal with the day-to-day in line with the overarching principles of the shared-parenting arrangement. In addition to this, ensure that you both agree with and understand the means by which you will handle the more serious or complex matters and ensure that you devote adequate time to this process.

Golden Rule #11 – Communication between you and your ex is CRITICAL to the successful maintenance of your shared-parenting. Ensure that you are able to discuss matters in a manner and with due consideration, time and sensitivity depending on the issue at hand.

Golden Rule #12 – Both of your children's places of residence should feel like and be treated as their homes. This sense should come about through both places being physically decorated to feel like home, with as few of their possessions following them about as possible to encourage a sense of permanence and belonging at both homes. A few basic principles can be adopted to ensure that the transit of 'things' between homes is kept to a minimum.

Golden Rule #13 – It is imperative that you protect and preserve the sanctity and structure of your shared-parenting arrangement as you would protect your kids themselves. Do not allow yourself to be swayed by others be they friends, family, new partners or acquaintances in terms of being forced to modify any aspect unless it is specifically for the benefit of the children. In this case, such changes should be discussed and agreed with the person whom you share the parenting with.

Golden Rule #14 – As you enter into new relationships, and indeed as you contemplate any major life changes, ensure that you are being 100% true to yourself and ensuring that you don't waver on the things that are essential to you in living the life you want. Failing to do this will impact upon your happiness as a person, and on your ability to be the parent that you want to be to your kids.

Embracing the spirit of the Golden Rules in the parenting of your kids will bring about great benefits in terms of their happiness, stability and wellbeing and will have equally positive effects in your own life as well.

If you are reading this in the hope of applying a shared-parenting structure for your own children, I hope that you will find the key lessons of the book simple to understand and easy to apply. It may be that you are reading this since you're intrigued about the concept of shared-parenting generally, or that you know someone (a friend or relative) who might be interested in putting a shared-parenting arrangement in place for the benefit of them and their children. That being the case I hope you will feel convinced enough to direct them towards this book. When I was first contemplating the world as a single parent I know I would have benefited from some sort of guide that if nothing else, offered me solace that there was a way of ensuring that I could still actively be involved in raising my daughters and see them on a regular basis. Shared-parenting is a very real and effective route to doing just that, and I heartily recommend it to anyone in a similar situation.

I wish you and your family great happiness in your lives.

About the Author

Toby Hazlewood is a father, husband, project manager, author and cycling enthusiast living in the North West of England. After a lifetime of largely ignoring kindly advice of others and failing to heed the many golden nuggets of wisdom offered to him, a mid-life existential crisis has prompted in him acknowledgement of this trait and a realization that he should change his ways and start writing down the lessons learned in the hope that others may avoid making the same mistakes he has.

Borne both of a genuine desire to help others, coupled with a tendency to over-analyse events from his past, Toby's writing documents experiences from his life-to-date and attempts to draw out lessons and learning points that are presented in a way that are easy to understand and simple to apply in the reader's life should they wish to. At the very least, he believes it may be of comfort to the reader to know that others that have shared experiences they have been through or are currently going through, and have come out the other side successfully.

Areas of focus and topics he has written on include:

- **Parenting** – As a single parent having raised two girls now aged 16 and 13 whose custody he shares 50-50 with their mother following a divorce, Toby has is keen to position shared-parenting as a model of the modern separated family that can be established for the benefit of children and parents alike.
- **Dating** – At the age of 30, a divorced father of two daughters, Toby launched himself on the online dating scene at the point it was just becoming popular. His experiences of the world of dating and relationships from this

period of life and his somewhat 'sparse' dating experience prior to marriage are shared with a self-effacing humour.

- **Health and Fitness** – At 186cm tall and with his weight ranging from 82KG to 111KG over the last 10 years, Toby has many lessons to share on how to manage your fitness, diet and body composition. His premise is that achieving manageable and enduring health and fitness is not reliant on a radical programme but rather on employment of common sense and being honest with yourself.
- **Personal Finance** – With a successful professional career that has spanned the dot-com boom and the subsequent bust, Toby has thoughts to share on how to make and manage money. He also has more than a few battle scars from mistakes and misjudgements made along the way.

Printed in Great Britain
by Amazon